ADELE DARLINGTON

SERIES EDITOR: EMMA TURNER

PRIMARY ART IN ACTION

IN ACTION SERIES

A **WALKTHRUs** PRODUCTION

hachette LEARNING

Together we unlock every learner's unique potential

At Hachette Learning (formerly Hodder Education), there's one thing we're certain about. No two students learn the same way. That's why our approach to teaching begins by recognising the needs of individuals first.

Our mission is to allow every learner to fulfil their unique potential by empowering those who teach them. From our expert teaching and learning resources to our digital educational tools that make learning easier and more accessible for all, we provide solutions designed to maximise the impact of learning for every teacher, parent and student.

Aligned to our parent company, Hachette Livre, founded in 1826, we pride ourselves on being a learning solutions provider with a global footprint.

www.hachettelearning.com

To order, please visit www.HachetteLearning.com or contact Customer Service at education@hachette.co.uk / +44 (0)1235 827827.

ISBN: 978 1 9152 6176 2

First published in 2026 by
Hachette Learning (a trading division of Hodder & Stoughton Limited),
An Hachette UK Company
Carmelite House
50 Victoria Embankment
London EC4Y 0DZ
www.HachetteLearning.com

The authorised representative in the EEA is Hachette Ireland, 8 Castlecourt Centre, Dublin 15, D15 XTP3, Ireland (email: info@hbgi.ie)

Impression number 10 9 8 7 6 5 4 3 2 1
Year 2030 2029 2028 2027 2026

Cover illustration by Oliver Caviglioli
Internal illustrations by DC Graphic Design Limited, Hextable, Kent.
Typeset in the UK.
Printed in the UK.

A catalogue record for this title is available from the British Library.

FSC www.fsc.org MIX Paper | Supporting responsible forestry FSC™ C104740

'As an artist, I believe that art in schools is essential – not just as a creative outlet, but as a powerful tool for personal development and expression. Art nurtures patience, focus and observation, qualities that have been central to my own journey. When pupils engage with drawing, painting or sculpture, they learn to see the world on a deeper level, to appreciate detail and to communicate emotions that words just sometimes can't express. Especially in today's fast-paced world, art gives young people a space to reflect, to build confidence and to discover their own unique voice. Every child deserves the opportunity to experience that.'

Kelvin Okafor, British-Nigerian Artist

SERIES FOREWORD

This series of books was commissioned as a *Walkthrus* production to complement two other series: the *Teaching Walkthrus* Volumes 1, 2 and 3 and the *In Action* series. Together the *Walkthrus* team believe the books create a powerful resource for teachers and leaders in schools.

The *In Action* series is very popular with busy teachers. These short, easy-to-read guides tackle important ideas from education, cognitive science and research, and translate the research findings into key ideas and approaches teachers can explore, adopt and implement in their own practice.

Designed to link research with real-world classroom applications, the *In Action* series provides an accessible outline of key theories that teachers can apply to their practice in their own unique settings.

- *Annie Murphy Paul's The Extended Mind in Action*
- *Ausubel's Meaningful Learning in Action*
- *Bandura's Self-Efficacy Theory in Action*
- *Collins et al's Cognitive Apprenticeship in Action*
- *Nuthall's Hidden Lives of Learners in Action*
- *Bjork & Bjork's Desirable Difficulties in Action*
- *Dunlosky's Strengthening the Student Toolbox in Action*
- *Berger's An Ethic of Excellence in Action*
- *Wiliam & Leahy's Five Formative Assessment Strategies in Action*
- *Shimamura's MARGE Model of Learning in Action*
- *Sweller's Cognitive Load Theory in Action*
- *Fiorella & Mayer's Generative Learning in Action*
- *Rosenshine's Principles in Action*
- *Engelmann's Direct Instruction in Action*

The writers of each of the *In Action* books are all either serving teachers or teachers who taught for many years; this means the books' foci are grounded in the reality of teaching pupils in real classrooms.

Alongside the *In Action* series, the three-volume *Teaching Walkthrus* series is another resource designed to support busy teachers, with research-informed practical classroom strategies. Over 35,000 copies have now been distributed worldwide, supported by the online *Walkthrus* toolkit.

Each *Walkthrus* book is designed in six main series. Each *Walkthru* is a context-free, visual five-step guide of ideas, techniques and approaches to be explored and applied in individual classrooms. They are designed to be adaptable, accessible and easy to use within training, coaching and personal reflection. The five steps provide, not a rigid structure or set of rules, but a framework for thinking through an idea, deconstructed so that teachers can reconstruct it themselves in their own unique classrooms to enact powerful techniques.

With the *In Action* series providing a bridge between research and practice, and the *Walkthrus* providing a framework for exploring and refining pedagogy, the *Subjects in Action* series (such as *Art in Action*) provides the third pillar: that of subject-specific support.

Each *In Action* subject book has been written by a primary subject expert who has sought to provide support, key information and ideas for subject leads and practising teachers in the primary phase. In primary, subject leads are often not subject specialists and colleagues are subject leads of more than one subject. This can be a real challenge for primary colleagues who are not immersed in a single subject discipline in the generalist primary classroom. These books are organised with a similar structure to their secondary counterparts so that primary teams can track key areas of focus across the whole series, making them easy to navigate and use as a connected suite of subject-lead resources.

It is no mean feat to capture the essence and spirit of a subject in a single volume and to balance the depth of detail of an entire subject community with a practical format to be used in multiple real-world classrooms.

These books are deliberately designed to be short in length but rich in support, practical advice and ideas, and all are written by highly experienced specialists who love their subjects and are passionate about practice in the primary phase.

This series is supportive enough for the non-specialist but rich enough to provide fresh avenues to explore for the experienced subject expert.

Editing the series has enabled me to see in sharp relief the unique beauty of each subject, brought skilfully to life by colleagues who truly love and champion their subject's place in the curriculum of our youngest children.

I hope you find this book and the wider series a professional friend – designed to help you develop your teaching and leading of each subject within the primary day. We have the opportunity in primary to accompany every pupil on their first steps into the formal academic disciplines; this book, I hope, is an invaluable companion when helping to plan the route.

Emma Turner

ABOUT THE AUTHOR

Adele Darlington is a Primary Art Education Consultant with over 24 years of classroom experience. Renowned for her inspiring and inclusive approach, Adele works globally to support pupils and teachers in unlocking creativity through art.

As well as writing the book *100 Ideas for Primary Teachers: Art*, published by Bloomsbury in 2022, Adele is a regular contributor to *Teach Primary* magazine. She is currently developing a progressive primary art curriculum with Haringey Education Partnership and regularly speaks at education conferences. She is currently an elected member of the National Society for Education in Art and Design Council.

Adele delivers hands-on workshops and training sessions, consistently receiving glowing feedback for her enthusiasm, deep subject knowledge and ability to inspire.

Passionate about promoting diversity and inclusion in the arts, Adele's work empowers schools to celebrate a broad range of voices and artistic traditions, ensuring every child sees themselves reflected in their learning.

ACKNOWLEDGEMENTS

I guess the place to start here is by thanking Leighfield Primary School, the place where I started my teaching career and stayed for a very long time! To the many (I'm too scared to say exactly how many for fear of sounding very old) children I've taught there, thank you for inspiring me and joining me on many art projects over the years. Steph and Sarah, thank you for putting up with my crazy arty ideas and trusting me to carry them out! I hope you enjoyed them as much as I did. Sorry I made a mess!

Thank you to the many contributors to this book from both the education world and art spaces. It wouldn't be what it is without your voices. I know teachers and schools will benefit from hearing your stories. I am extremely grateful for your input and support for this project.

To Mum, Dad, Hannah and Coco, thank you for making me cups of tea and encouraging me when I came to stay with my laptop. Thanks Dad, for breaking up my writing time sharing your magic tricks and telling me the new jokes you'd heard on the radio!

And last but by no means least, Shaun, Lewis, Mia and Henry. Thank you, thank you, thank you for putting up with me through thick and thin, highs and lows. The writing journey is no easy task and you've all been my rocks throughout the process. I love you to the moon and back, infinity times.

REVIEWS

Just like a piece of art that you want to see again and again, *Primary Art in Action* is a book you'll revisit time and time again. I love it. Why? It is packed with practical guidance, research-informed approaches and creative ideas. No matter what your starting point – teaching art for the first time, an art subject leader or senior leader – Adele's awesome and accessible book will help you create the best art curriculum and lessons to inspire every learner.

Sophie Leach, FRSA, AD magazine, Editor; NSEAD Deputy General Secretary

Primary Art in Action is a superbly practical, inspiring and authoritative guide that captures the rigour, joy and transformative power of primary art. It moves expertly from big ideas, research and progression to planning, assessment, sketchbooks and curriculum enrichment. Adele's work shines with deep subject expertise, inclusive conviction and a powerful belief that every child can see themselves as an artist.

Steve Varnam, Director of Quality Assurance & School Improvement, Flying High Partnership

A brilliant resource, *Primary Art in Action* is essential reading for primary practitioners. It beautifully combines the latest research with case studies, example planning sequences and creative art project ideas. Crucially, the book tackles common misconceptions and has diversity and inclusivity at its core.

Shareen Wilkinson, Author, Curriculum and English Specialist and Chief Education Officer, LEO Academy Trust

From developing curiosity in art through its big questions to how to use a sketchbook in the classroom, this book is a must for any primary teacher. It's an easily accessible, practical guide on how to teach art and is rooted in current pedagogical thinking. *Primary Art in Action* skilfully and clearly sets out the expectations of a primary art & design curriculum and guides teachers to achieve success in their settings with endless practical ideas to engage and support pupils. This book will make absolutely anybody excited about teaching this subject! Here, Adele shows she is a leading thinker in the teaching of primary art.

Heather De Silva, Lead for Professional Development, Haringey Education Partnership

Primary Art in Action is one of those books you'll keep reaching for. It's full of thoughtful insights, practical ideas and moments that make you reflect on your own practice, whatever stage of your career you're at. Adele has a real gift for making complex ideas feel accessible without oversimplifying them, and her passion for high quality, inclusive art education shines through. Whether you're a class teacher wanting to build confidence in teaching art or an experienced art subject lead looking to strengthen your curriculum, you'll find lots of value here. This book is informative, inspiring and fun to read. An essential addition to any collection of art education books.

Emily Gopaul, Art Education Consultant and Art & Design Lead at Oak National Academy

Art is one of those subjects that has the power to change how children see the world – and how they see themselves. Adele has captured that beautifully. This isn't just another book about teaching art; it's a practical, thoughtful and inspiring guide that helps teachers and leaders understand why art matters just as much as how to teach it well. Every chapter is rooted in the reality of primary schools, with ideas that are immediately usable without losing sight of the bigger picture. Whether you're an experienced subject leader or someone lacking confidence in teaching art, this book will leave you feeling more knowledgeable, more inspired and ready to give children the rich artistic experiences they deserve. An outstanding addition to every primary school's professional library.

Halil Tamgumus, School Improvement Advisor,
Discovery Schools Academies Trust

Having read *Primary Art in Action*, I can honestly say it is an inspiring, practical and much-needed resource for anyone involved in primary education. The book successfully combines educational expertise with a genuine passion for creativity, making it both informative and engaging from start to finish. What impressed me most was its accessibility. Guidance is clear, supportive and relevant whether you are a specialist art teacher, a subject leader or a classroom teacher looking to develop confidence in teaching art. Adele presents ideas in a way that feels achievable while still encouraging ambition and high expectations for pupils. The practical examples, planning support and curriculum guidance are particularly valuable. Rather than simply discussing theory, the book provides actionable strategies that can be implemented in real classroom settings. It offers a thoughtful balance between developing artistic skills, nurturing creativity and helping children build confidence in expressing themselves through art. There is a strong emphasis on inclusion, diversity and representation, recognising the importance of ensuring that every child sees themselves reflected within the curriculum while also being introduced to a broad range of artists, cultures and creative perspectives. This commitment to equity and belonging is woven throughout the text and strengthens its educational impact. It is not just a guide to teaching art; it is a reminder of the profound impact that creative opportunities can have on children's learning, wellbeing and sense of identity.

Christalla Jamil FCCT, Chief Executive Officer,
LDBS Academies Trust

Crafting and designing a high-quality Primary Art curriculum can be challenging. On my travels around schools, I see much variance in the quality of art curricula. The reasons for this rarely stem from a school's lack of trying. Instead, it often comes down to a lack of deep subject knowledge and that overwhelming 'where do I begin?' sensation in a teacher's or subject leader's mind. This is exactly why *Primary Art in Action* is an essential read for anyone in the primary education world. It demystifies all aspects of how to craft and deliver an excellent primary art curriculum. Adele achieves this by sharing her vast wisdom in bite-sized chunks of information, backed up by plenty of real-life examples. It is a true 'pick up and go' resource for busy teachers and leaders. Adele has given us a window into her amazing mind! What a triumph!

Sarah Sadler, Director of Sadler Education Advisory Services

CONTENTS

Series Editor's introduction 1

Introduction: The big picture: Art 3

Chapter 1 Big Ideas 10

Chapter 2 Debates and perspectives 21

Chapter 3 Subject-specific research 27

Chapter 4 Age progression 36

Chapter 5 Sample planning sequence 69

Chapter 6 Core and hinterland 90

Chapter 7 Difficult concepts and misconceptions 96

Chapter 8 Mode A and Mode B 105

Chapter 9 Sample lessons 111

Chapter 10 Assessment 124

Chapter 11 Products and projects 145

Chapter 12 Links with other subjects 154

Acknowledgements 160

SERIES EDITOR'S INTRODUCTION

This is the book I wish I'd had as a primary-school class teacher. Art is a subject that often feels like something you either can or can't do, be that as someone trying to produce your own artwork or trying to teach art to young pupils. Often it can be relegated to the afternoon session later in the week that actually then never comes or is reduced to 30 identikit copies of famous paintings across every classroom in the school with a few celebration cards and a brief encounter with clay in one brave year group. It can be seen as expensive to resource, chaotic to teach, hard to assess and, frankly, terrifying to teach as a non-specialist – that is, until you read this book.

Adele's love for the subject, and her vast and detailed knowledge of art, artists and what works with primary-age pupils, has provided this ultimate *Walkthru* of why, what and how to teach primary art with confidence, clarity and passion. I have learned more about primary art through editing this book than I have in decades of class teaching and school leadership. Adele's skilful assimilation of voices from the art world, pupils' own reflections on their art learning and a wide range of examples from schools and trusts of contrasting size, approach and structure mean that this is a resource that will resonate with both the non-specialist teacher and the seasoned art-subject lead.

Through Adele's vast experience and obvious passion for what art can do for our youngest learners, she outlines how to build a school and an approach that champions and nurtures the artist in everyone. Her deep and thoughtful discussion of the important role that art plays in the lives of our children and their communities, and the expressive and transformative power of art, means that this book not only leaves you empowered to plan a well-sequenced curriculum but eager to put art firmly back at the centre of pupils' primary-school experience.

Simple and clear guides through progression, planning, assessment and subject knowledge sit alongside rich and diverse recommendations, commentary and championing of art as not only a statutory part of our national curriculum but an essential part of the human experience.

This is a masterclass in how to love your subject and convey that love to others in a way that makes them feel not only that they want to, but that they can.

Picasso said the famous words 'Every child is an artist'. However, few know the second part of that quotation: 'The problem is how to remain an artist once we grow up.' Having had the privilege of editing this book, I think that Adele's writing means that that problem might just be well on the way to being solved.

Emma Turner

INTRODUCTION
THE BIG PICTURE: ART

Informed by experience of teaching in the classroom, research into curriculum design and subject pedagogy, this book provides a simple and inspiring vision for primary art and design. It offers insight and guidance for anyone wanting to develop art as a rigorous and joyful subject founded on practical knowledge, theoretical understanding and disciplinary awareness. From the class teacher who wants to develop their art teaching practice or skills, and the dedicated art lead who wants to develop their school's curriculum, to the senior leader wanting to ensure high-quality provision across the key stages, this book provides practical guidance rooted in principle to ensure that every pupil becomes a confident artist.

The chapters develop this guidance as follows:

- **Chapter 1** sets out the Big Ideas that underpin primary art and design. By establishing the wider areas of identity, communication and representation, this chapter helps you to show pupils how topics link together, developing subject mastery and revealing art and design as more than the sum of its topics.
- **Chapter 2** explores the debates that characterise primary art and design. Analysing claims around modelling; convergent versus divergent outcomes; and process versus product, this chapter helps you navigate these questions and arrive at decisions that work for you and your context.
- **Chapter 3** surveys recent research into primary art and design teaching and learning, pulling together and distilling accessible, practical knowledge from key studies including the Ofsted Research Review, the Art-K survey and the RAPS project.
- **Chapter 4** unpacks the national curriculum statements for art and design, breaking down each clause and demonstrating what is required at KS1 and 2 so you can plan for progression through the primary phase.
- **Chapter 5** models the processes involved in planning a sequence of learning, from the overview down to individual lessons. Framed by a worked example, Exploring Colour with Year 1 pupils, this chapter

helps you see how subject knowledge, skills and creative exploration can be taught side by side.

- **Chapter 6** explores the role of the curriculum hinterland in art and design lessons. Utilising Christine Counsell's framework of core and hinterland knowledge, this chapter helps you identify ways to bring key art and design concepts to life.
- **Chapter 7** unpicks confusing concepts in art and design, addressing common misconceptions and problem areas for pupils and teachers alike so that you can plan lessons with confidence and ensure subject knowledge really sinks in for pupils.
- **Chapter 8** analyses the parallels between Tom Sherrington's ideas on Mode A and Mode B teaching and applies this to the primary art classroom. Exploring where teacher modelling and pupil investigation can each play a role in your teaching space, this chapter helps you strike a balance between technical knowledge and creative exploration.
- **Chapter 9** offers a range of worked sample lessons that can form the foundation for planning your own art and design lessons. Bringing together the theory from previous chapters, this chapter models these principles in action across the primary age range.
- **Chapter 10** focuses specifically on assessing pupils' learning in art and design. Recognising the challenges posed by the subjective elements of this creative subject, this chapter helps you find a balance of assessment techniques that meets both pupils' and schools' needs.
- **Chapter 11** explores ways to enrich your school's art and design offer beyond regular lessons. From assemblies to termly initiatives, and after-school clubs to whole-school projects, this chapter helps you identify ways of celebrating and promoting art and design around your school.
- **Chapter 12** shows how to incorporate art into every area of the curriculum. Finding links between art and design and music, history, science and English, this chapter helps you ensure pupils make cross-curricular connections as they learn about art.

What is art?

Art is a beautiful subject: one that adds colour, culture and an unrivalled richness to the world both for its creators and admirers. But what actually is it?

While planning out the contents for this book, I thought this introduction would be the easiest section to write. I talk about art all the time, so surely it wouldn't take long to talk about what it actually is. In fact, the more I considered it, the more elusive a definition became, its many branches and benefits impossible to pack into a simple explanation. I opened the dictionary to see whether that would help, but it gave only a tiny and restrictive view of the subject – a mention of painting and drawing with a smidge of creativity. Such a simplistic definition of art does not do the subject justice, describing it only on a surface level. But, if we dig deeper, we find a greater breadth of areas of making, as well as an understanding of the communicative and expressive power of art, with an immeasurable number of cognitive and academic benefits. So, let's attempt to go further and think about the subject's scope, its meaning and its place in the world.

I asked an incredible group of colleagues, friends and ex-pupils to help me here by describing what art means to them, because art is a deeply personal phenomenon and should be recognised and celebrated as such. To give you just my voice would not be in keeping with the subjective nature of art. It means different things to different people; no matter how hard we try, we will never find one, simple and definitive answer to this overarching question.

The responses from these contributors vary, but the message at the heart of all of them is the same: art plays a beautiful, powerful, important and impactful role in our lives. It has a transformative power, not only as a visual experience, but as a vessel for social awareness, healing and change.

So, read each of these quotations in turn carefully, digest them slowly, then ask yourself the same questions: What is art and what does it mean to you?

> *What is art? It's a drawing of a dancing woman or a painting of thin asparagus lying on the table; it's a woodblock print of a crashing wave, or a large red lobster suspended on a telephone! From everyday scenes to cataclysmic events and funny moments in between, art makes me look! It draws my attention to the world, helping me to slow down and appreciate its shapes, colours, objects, places and people. Above all, my favourite artworks make me feel a sense of wonder.*
>
> **Ruth Millington, Art Historian, Curator and Author**

> *Art is something that looks nice. It could be a painting, drawing, sticking and cutting things. It could be made from fabric or even singing and dancing! Art makes me feel happy, energetic, giggly, screamy and shouty because I can do it in whatever way I want to do it, and I can be free with nobody to tell me what to do with it.*
>
> **Sidney Taylor-Pettener, age 6**

> *Art is everything and nothing, revealed or concealed, fleeting yet eternal. It transforms the mundane into the beautiful, the benign into the shocking. It is a uniquely human impulse, a fickle and restless force that frustrates as often as it astounds. Art refuses to be pinned down, yet it is always there, waiting to be seen, felt and reimagined.*
>
> **Stuart Jarvis, Secondary Teacher, Former Director of Art and Artist**

Art gives us the opportunity to communicate without the need for words; to be free, use our imaginations and represent our thoughts and feelings visually and without fear of judgement. It's a place to escape, whether that be when creating it or getting lost in the work of others.

Indeed, art is fun, art is varied and art brings smiles, but it is important to acknowledge and remember that it is also a highly skilled and technical subject. Art is not a subject just for those who are non-academic, despite this dated stigma being attached to it. Often, art in schools is viewed as that 'leave it for a supply', 'what shall we do on Friday afternoon?', 'quick, we need something for a wall display!' kind of subject but, if pupils are to be given the high-quality art education they deserve, it is essential that schools research and craft out a carefully sequenced, quality programme of study. Art is not an afterthought, but an important, fundamental component of primary education. Art is not only the painting of a pretty picture; it's the crafting and honing of a multitude of discipline-specific skills alongside the absorption of the knowledge of art history and art now.

Inspiring the next generation of creatives

So, why is art essential in our schools and what do we want pupils to learn? The national curriculum for KS1 and KS2 Art and Design Purpose of Study sums this up concisely:

> *Art, craft and design embody some of the highest forms of human creativity. A high-quality art and design education should engage, inspire*

and challenge pupils, equipping them with the knowledge and skills to experiment, invent and create their own works of art, craft and design. As pupils progress, they should be able to think critically and develop a more rigorous understanding of art and design. They should also know how art and design both reflect and shape our history, and contribute to the culture, creativity and wealth of our nation.

DfE, 2013

It then goes on to state that, during their time in primary school, pupils should:

- *produce creative work, exploring their ideas and recording their experiences*
- *become proficient in drawing, painting, sculpture and other art, craft and design techniques*
- *evaluate and analyse creative works using the language of art, craft and design*
- *know about great artists, craft makers and designers, and understand the historical and cultural development of their art forms.*

Primary schools and the teachers within them have a collective responsibility to start pupils off on their artistic journeys with excitement, enthusiasm and passion. Art and design is a subject that can bring joy to the curriculum but can also help make sense of the world, illustrate concepts and represent ideas and feelings visually. An early love of art can set individuals off on a rewarding path towards a creative career. The study of art does not lead only to artists creating paintings for admiration in a gallery, but a real plethora of exciting job roles. Society needs its creative workforce to thrive, and the future makers and creators are in our classrooms now!

Aside from this, it's also important to consider the benefits to wellbeing that art and design can bring. When discussing the subject with a selection of pupils in my school, so many of them mentioned the freeing, calming, relaxing effect that engaging in the subject brings them. 'It's that happy let go' was the response of a pupil in Year 4, a quotation that beautifully sums up the comforting power of art: a subject in which pupils can be themselves, rather than like everybody else.

Artist identities

If the aim of the primary art and design experience is to equip pupils with the confidence, knowledge and skills to work as individual artists, it is important to instil early on the understanding that art is vastly varied and deeply subjective. What one person likes can vary greatly from the next person. Likewise, one person's artistic strengths and style can vary enormously from another's. This does not mean that one is correct and the other incorrect, or that one is more talented and more likely to pursue a career in the art world. Artists do not have to be and look a certain way. All art should be valued, and all preferences respected and accepted. It's important that all adults working with pupils on their artist journeys support, understand and encourage this mindset. Confidence is one of the biggest barriers to artistic success, so the earlier pupils believe in the validity of their own artistic responses and uniqueness the better. Every pupil should have their imagination and artistic expression celebrated and nurtured. This is essential to their personal progression and evolution as an artist. Primary schools and teachers have the responsibility of igniting a passion for art and design in their pupils. Once lit, they have the important and somewhat complex task of keeping it burning so that pupils want to create and immerse themselves in the subject, no matter their skillset, ability or knowledge.

In the same way as we encourage an appreciation of individual reader identities when encouraging reading for pleasure, it is of the utmost importance that we celebrate every pupil's identity as an artist. As with reading, enjoyment in art is deeply personal. So, how can we find out and respect each pupil's likes, dislikes, interests and styles? Over time, teachers get to know their pupils, but there are also dedicated activities that can help to speed up the process. One obvious way is to find time to talk and listen to pupils about their likes and dislikes. This could be a discussion-based or a sketchbook activity allowing pupils the freedom to share their stories in any way they wish. Teachers can join in; pupils enjoy listening to the adults in the room sharing their ideas too, although it's important to remember that the aim of this process is to encourage pupils to think for (and of) themselves and not be swayed by the thoughts and feelings of others.

Use the following questions as prompts to enable pupils to share their thoughts:

- What type of art do you like to look at?

- How does art make you feel?
- Do you have a favourite artist?
- Which tools and media do you like to use?
- Where do you like to create?
- When do you like to create?
- Do you like to create from observation or imagination?
- What helps you to create?

Pupils love to reflect on their 'artist identity' sketchbook pages, both throughout the academic year and year on year. Many see changes and progression in themselves as artists as their knowledge of the subject grows and their experiences widen. This sort of discussion should not be kept as a 'one-off' activity, but woven throughout the curriculum, developing a culture of art talk, individual expression and empathy.

When pupils come to see themselves as artists in their own right, the work of primary art and design has truly begun. The chapters that follow are a guide to nurturing and sustaining that work in every primary classroom.

Further reading

'Discover! Creative Careers' on Inspiring the Future [online] Available at: www.inspiringthefuture.org/campaigns/discover-creative-careers (Accessed: 14 May 2026).

Millington, R. (2022) *Muse: Uncovering the Hidden Figures Behind Art History's Masterpieces*. London: Square Peg.

NSEAD (2024) 'Manifesto for Art, Craft and Design Education'. Corsham: National Society for Education in Art and Design [online] Available at: www.nsead.org (Accessed: 14 May 2026).

Ofsted (2023) 'Research review series: art and design' [online] Available at: www.gov.uk/government/publications/research-review-series-art-and-design (Accessed: 14 May 2026).

CHAPTER 1
BIG IDEAS

When people talk about Big Ideas in a subject, what do they actually mean? Put simply, they're referring to the overarching themes in a particular field. It is under the umbrella of these Big Ideas that pupils are able to make links between individual concepts and the different elements of the curriculum they experience in school. Big Ideas aren't taught in isolation; they underpin the whole curriculum. Pupils develop an understanding of them through the careful curation of curriculum building-blocks alongside wider, subject-specific experiences. In the case of art and design, these could be such enhancements as gallery or museum visits, artist-residency programmes, visits from local artists or art competitions.

This chapter explores some of the Big Ideas in art and design, of which there are many to choose from. The elements of art materials and techniques associated with the subject are purposefully omitted, as these feature in Chapter 5. Those discussed here are ones that have meaning and relevance for pupils in a primary school, just starting out on their journeys as artists. They help to develop a comprehensive understanding of the subject. Alongside these Big Ideas, the subject of art and design incorporates some unique ways of working that distinguish it far from other subjects on the primary curriculum; notably, creativity and the use of sketchbooks.

Let's explore some of art's Big Ideas.

Art is...

... a window

Art is a window into the world. Through it, individuals can be taken to different places and spaces, whether it be with Claude Monet to the gardens of Giverny or with Georgia O'Keeffe to the landscapes of New Mexico. It is also a vessel for transcending time: viewers of artworks can travel forwards or backwards through the ages or choose to pause and stand still in the present. Art awakens the senses and opens eyes to new perspectives, to new ways of seeing things that are seemingly already known, as well as teaching about things that are not. Art gives everyone an equal chance to read and make sense of the world, without the need for words, which are an accessibility barrier for so many.

… a communicator

Is there a more powerful form of communication than art? The way it transcends language barriers and cultural differences sets it apart from all other methods. Art communicates ideas, emotions, experiences, messages and stories through a visual language all of its own. It connects individuals, both artists and viewers, and encourages conversation.

Artists demonstrate this in countless ways, using their practice to educate, challenge, connect and bear witness. Kelvin Okafor's *Drawing Awareness* series was developed with the intention of educating and encouraging an understanding of and empathy towards individuals with visible differences, communicating their stories to a wider audience. Tan Zi Xi raises awareness of ocean pollution through her sculptures and detailed illustrations. Her installation piece 'Plastic Ocean' (2016) was made from over 20,000 pieces of plastic rubbish that were collected in Mumbai. Through her works, she aims to communicate the worrying reality of plastic consumption and disposal.

Some artists use their practice as a way of communicating visually what they find hard to do in words. They use techniques and elements of art to illustrate their feelings. The same can be said for pupils in the classroom: art is a way for them to express how they feel in a non-intrusive way, in their own time and space.

… history

This Big Idea can be seen as twofold. On the one hand, there is the history of art; the timeline of art movements, artworks and artists across centuries that have paved the way for now. On the other hand, there is the role art plays in teaching us *about* history; its role as a historical artefact. Way back before the time of the photograph, artists captured moments in time that inform us of all aspects of life during different periods the world over.

… inspiration

Art has a way of inspiring. Looking at an artwork can stir emotions, inspire discussions and stimulate creativity. Comparing and contrasting artwork not only expands the artistic repertoire of individuals, but it also gives them a bank of ideas to use as inspiration for their own explorations. Art inspires pupils in art and design lessons, and can also excite pupils across the whole curriculum.

... an exploration of identity

Many artists use the medium of art to explore and understand themselves, producing work expressing their own unique identities, personal experiences, family life and cultural backgrounds, among other aspects of their lives. Some create self-portraits or portraits, such as Amoako Boafo's works celebrating black identity. Others use alternative imagery to represent themselves and their narratives, such as Tim Fowler, who created a body of work entitled *The Ground*, exploring his Bajan heritage through a study of plants that have taken a similar migratory journey to his own DNA.

... representation

The picture book *Parker Looks Up: An Extraordinary Moment* by Parker Curry, Jessica Curry and Brittany Jackson (Aladdin, 2019) perfectly illustrates this Big Idea, telling the true story of a young girl, Parker Curry, and the moment she came face to face with Amy Sherald's portrait of Michelle Obama at the National Portrait Gallery in Washington DC. A photo of Curry went viral on the internet after a fellow gallery visitor took a photo of her looking up in awe at the large-scale portrait. The painting captured the young girl's attention as she connected with Obama: she saw not only a painting, but she also saw herself and her possibilities and dreams.

Art has the power to make these connections, to allow people to feel seen and represented.

Comfort for creativity

Artists work in any way, shape or form that allows their skills and creativity to flow. They need to be comfortable. Depending on task and scale, they may work sitting, standing or even lying on the floor. These habits and conventions of creating art can easily be transferred to the classroom, even though they don't fit with the traditional expectations of seating and working arrangements.

In art and design sessions, pupils are working as artists – if they create most comfortably standing, let them stand. If they want to sit or lie and work on the floor, then so be it. While this approach may not be conducive to work in a maths lesson or for carrying out a SATs paper, in the world of art it fits perfectly. Monet stood to paint his world-famous waterlily creations; Pollock stood and bent over his canvases to create his infamous splatter paintings. Pupils need to be comfortable and at ease for optimum creation to occur.

Using sketchbooks

Sketchbooks play a fundamental role in the art experience of primary-school pupils. Mentioned in the key stage 2 national curriculum Programmes of Study, they are a place for pupils to keep a record of their journey through the subject. Despite their name and dictionary definition, sketchbooks aren't just for sketching in; they are a place to explore all media and techniques, and a more useful name for them would perhaps be an *art book* or *art journal*. In an ideal classroom setup, these books should be kept close to hand to allow pupils the opportunity to reach into them to record their thoughts and feelings, explore, discover, rehearse and experiment with new ideas.

There are a variety of different sketchbooks available for schools to purchase, with an ascending scale of price points. The big educational suppliers stock a selection, and specialist art suppliers offer high-quality products for schools too. Books vary in size, orientation and quality, so it's beneficial to shop around, discuss experiences of other schools and even order samples to explore before committing to a big whole-school order. When selecting sketchbooks, it's important to consider the quality of the pages within them. Unlike an exercise book, these pages need to be able to handle both wet and dry media and the application of varying pressure with different tools. If budget is an issue, some schools have pupils make their own sketchbooks using a variety of paper types found around school. However you select or create your sketchbooks, they are an integral and essential part of the art and design curriculum and central to working as an artist.

Sketchbooks are the art and design lesson equivalent of an exercise book, but they are not exercise books. There are a number of profound differences and expectations between use of the two. These differences are easier to understand when we consider the purpose of a sketchbook. The ultimate goal of the primary art and design curriculum is to create confident individual artists; to equip them with a technically proficient skillset to make their own artistic choices. The sketchbook is their safe space to experiment, explore and try out new ideas; it's also a place to rehearse and refine techniques, free from a fear of failure or judgement. Artist Grayson Perry spoke of his sketchbook habit in an interview with

The Guardian newspaper (2016) and summed up sketchbooks with this notion: 'between the covers I feel safe – the drawings need never be seen by anyone but me – and thus I can play'. While the school setup is not quite the same as Perry's studio, the goal is the same: to create a comfortable space in which to create.

If sketchbooks are used in this way, they become physical manifestations of a pupil's thinking. Pages do not simply contain finished pieces; they provide insight into the planning that led to those pieces, the starting points that became sidetracked, ideas altered and re-altered as decisions are considered and, most importantly, the thoughts of the pupil as they evaluate their own work. This is metacognition in action: pupils thinking about their learning through planning their work, monitoring their own understanding and evaluating their outputs. The Education Endowment Foundation (2025) estimates metacognition and self-regulation as some of the highest-impact, lowest-cost interventions, resulting in pupils making an average of eight months' additional progress over a year. The sketchbook provides one of the most natural environments for this learning to take place.

So, how can teachers work towards creating this confident 'have a go' culture in their classrooms? The first step is to treat the sketchbooks in their own unique way. Habits commonly associated with exercise books just don't fit with the safe space required for optimum art experiences and confidence to flow. Some common features and expectations of exercise-book use follow, with accompanying considerations for sketchbooks.

Exercise-book expectations

Learning objectives evident for each new piece of work

A pupil's notes and annotations on a page should indicate the learning that has taken place. There is no real need for a learning objective if this is the case. Some schools choose to stick sequence overviews, which outline the subsequent learning that happens, in sketchbooks at the beginning of a new unit of work. Remember: time in art lessons is short and precious; if pupils are going to spend precious minutes writing out objectives, is this the best use of their creative time?

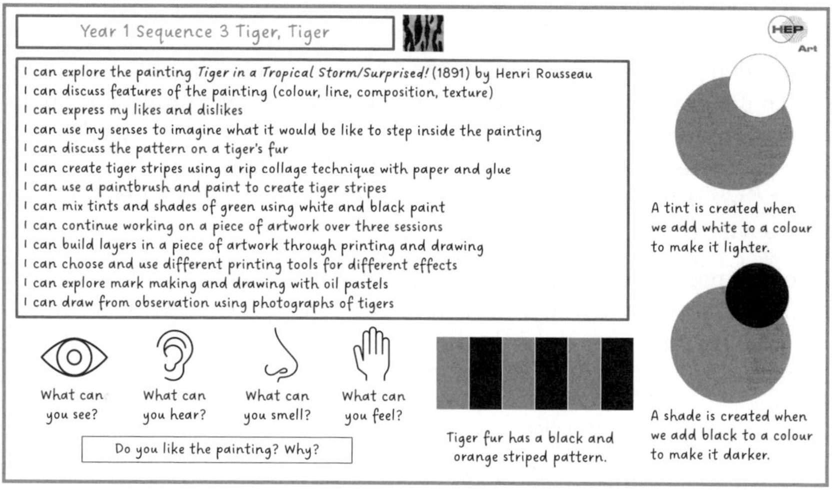

▲ **Figure 1.1 Example of a sequence overview (Haringey Education Partnership)**

Traditional methods of presentation (date, miss a line, title, miss a line, start!)

In a sketchbook, anything goes! Headings can be placed anywhere, as can doodles, explorations, annotations, notes. It is up to individual artists how and where they arrange their thoughts and feelings on the page.

Neatness at all times

Sketchbooks aren't 'best' books, or books of perfect drawings and paintings. They are spaces to explore, to try out new techniques and media, to stop and start again; a place to refine skills, experiment and play. Sketchbooks with drips, paint splashes, charcoal smudges, ink stains and more demonstrate immersion in the subject and an embracing of exploration – most definitely not carelessness or lack of pride. Rubbers aren't needed to rub out: mistakes are good to see, and a pupil's responses to them are even better. They help demonstrate a pupil's artistic journey and progress.

Writing in NSEAD's *AD* magazine, artist and lecturer Simone Maier (2025) describes sketchbook practice as 'smelly research': work that values exploratory thinking and personal meaning over polished outcomes. Although Maier writes about higher-education students, the principle holds in the primary classroom too.

Books look similar as all pupils carry out the same task

Art and design lessons are lessons about individuality and creativity. When we give pupils too strict a formula to follow, we limit their ability to think creatively. Some pupils need guidance to begin their work, while others thrive off being able to show what they know, how they feel and what they discover in their own unique way. A sketchbook should be a space where they can take risks.

Ken Robinson (2017) reminds us that creativity is predicated on making mistakes; if we cultivate a classroom environment that punishes pupils for making mistakes, we are training them out of experimentation that is necessary for creating original work.

Accurate spelling and punctuation

It is hoped that pupils apply their spelling, grammar and punctuation knowledge across all areas of the curriculum, but what do these skills inform teachers of a pupil's artistic ability or thinking? Is it really essential to demand accuracy in this area in a sketchbook? By insisting pupils revisit and correct errors, teachers may be interrupting creative flow and 'spoiling' the look and feel of sketchbook pages.

Teacher marking and feedback evident

Teacher feedback in art lessons is important, but it doesn't necessarily need to be in the form of pen on paper. Sketchbook pages are works of art so, with that in mind, is it right to make marks on someone else's artwork and change the look and feel of their explorations, discoveries and creations? If evidence of feedback is required, sticky notes can be used to avoid defacing the actual pages, or a section of the page (maybe a bottom corner) marked out and left blank for this purpose.

Artists' sketchbooks

When it comes to content and purpose, a look inside the sketchbook pages of current or historical artists can prove an inspiration both to pupils and their teachers. Such pages can clarify expectations and help individuals make sense of the intentions of their use. A search for an artist's name and 'sketchbook' brings up plentiful hits to choose from. The anatomical drawings of Leonardo da Vinci surrounded by notes and annotations; Frida Kahlo's experimentations and playfulness with colour; Van Gogh's exploration and rehearsal of form; Paul Cézanne's rough pencil-sketch landscapes; Grayson Perry's exploration of composition; Charles Darwin's scientific recordings – all clearly demonstrate to pupils the varying uses and invaluable purposes of a sketchbook.

> During my long career, I have probably filled over 100 sketchbooks and, unlike my paintings, I have kept every single one of them. They are a valuable resource and provide a wealth of ideas and also act as a diary, recording my modes of working and the events taking place in my life at that time. In the early days, I would use them to plan compositions for my still lifes and to record landscapes on location, often using written notes detailing colour, light source, tone and texture. Some immediately formed the basis of a studio painting and some have inspired work 20 years later.
>
> I often use a sketchbook when I visit exhibitions, as it requires more concentrated looking than a camera. I use sketchbooks to experiment in using different media, such as collage, gesso, random brushwork, print techniques, etc. building layers and abstracting the subject. I find when I am working on a small, intimate scale I am much braver and can happily 'play' for hours without the pressure of producing a finished work. These experiments, and many failures, help build confidence and develop skills to push my practice forwards. As well as traditional sketchbooks, I have made use of a concertina format, especially when on location. This allows you to travel with a small A5 book, which, when extended, has 72 faces to work on as it is double sided. It is both convenient and challenging in its format and has resulted in many long, thin, rectangular paintings.
>
> To see an artist's sketchbook is to see a very personal side of their thought process; it is where the germ of an idea can grow and develop, or where it can simply fizzle out.
>
> **Jenny Grevatte, Artist**
> **www.jennygrevatte.co.uk**

Sketchbooks for research

In the classroom, pupils can use sketchbooks to record their research on artists, art movements and media. On the same pages, they can annotate and express their likes and dislikes, and their individual thoughts and feelings on what they have found. They can try out techniques inspired by artists or modelled by the teacher; they can rehearse, refine, make links and apply what they know. They can explore 'what happens if' moments, articulate their findings, and more. Evaluation is a constant thread that can run through sketchbook use, either in the form of notes on the paper or rich in dialogue in class. Artists are constantly evaluating their work, from the first mark on a page through to a finished piece, and it is a valuable skill to develop in pupils as they deepen their understanding of art as a subject and develop themselves as artists.

Teacher sketchbooks can be a valuable tool in supporting, encouraging and inspiring pupils. As the term suggests, these are books – the same as ones pupils use – but belonging to their teachers: a place for teachers to prepare example pages if required, and to sit alongside pupils, creating in the moment with them. Developing a sketchbook habit takes time, and having a teacher model using one can be powerful. Teachers can model thinking processes out loud, promote a growth-mindset attitude, create discussion points, set standards of expectation and model starting points for those reluctant to make a mark.

Sketchbooks in schools

During my time as Art Lead at Leighfield Primary School, every pupil from Year 1 through to Year 6 was given a sketchbook; the national curriculum mentions their use only in KS2 but many schools, like ours, choose for pupils to use them from Year 1. The books were kept easily accessible in classrooms for pupils to reach for and use. The sketchbooks were kept solely for art and design content and weren't a mix of learning in other curriculum areas – we had separate files for design and technology. I mention this subject specifically because, on my travels around schools, I often see these two discrete subjects (with many crossovers) blurred together; when this happens, it seems the profile of each gets watered down and devalued. Pupils used their sketchbooks to rehearse skills, make discoveries, create, explore, experiment, record research, record their thoughts and feelings, evaluate and reflect. They were given freedom to choose the way they presented their pages, and the books were as unique as the pupils they belonged to.

On the inside front cover of the sketchbooks, we stuck evaluation and reflection prompts for pupils to refer to during lessons. This helped them to work independently and constantly evaluate the art processes they were exploring. Questions were along the lines of:

- What are you creating?
- What inspired you?
- What could you do next?

- Which materials and techniques are you using?
- What have you discovered?
- How do you feel about the end result?
- What do you like or dislike about it?
- What would you like to explore more of?
- Did you encounter any problems?
- How did you overcome them?

To help pupils further with writing and speaking about art, we had a vocabulary mat stuck onto the inside of the back cover. This not only helped pupils as a reference when articulating themselves as artists, but also teachers, especially those less confident in the teaching of the subject. It was a useful reference point to find vocabulary associated with the different elements of art.

Due to the unique nature of sketchbook use, some schools write a sketchbook policy for staff and pupils to follow in their settings, the aim of this being to support those teachers less confident in art and design and to ensure consistency of use across the school. Consistency helps pupil understanding of expectations and gives them the opportunity to develop their own sketchbook habits.

If sketchbooks are kept well, they provide evidence of a pupil's journey through a subject. We can see their progression not just through blocks of lessons but from year to year. We can flick through their sketchbook to see them trying out techniques, developing them and then applying them to new projects, with their own artistic voice developing along the way.

Summary

The questions I've attempted to answer in this chapter – What is art for? Why does it matter? How can sketchbooks help us teach art as a discipline rooted in experimentation, reflection and finding your own voice? – are the bedrock on which everything else is built. The following three chapters delve deeper into the curricular, pedagogical and progression aspects of primary art and design in turn, but each is built on the beliefs I've outlined here; that children are artists, that our subject is as rigorous as it is creative and that a well-taught primary-art curriculum provides every pupil with the knowledge, skills and confidence to create art that is meaningful to them.

Further reading

Gomersal Primary School Art Blog [online] Available at: https://gomersalprimaryschoolart.blogspot.com (Accessed: 14 May 2026).

Grevatte, J. (2025) *Beyond Brushstrokes*. Uppingham: Goldmark.

Maier, S. (2025) 'Sketchbooks: Play in pursuit of an unknown outcome' in *AD* The National Society for Education in Art and Design magazine), Summer 2025, Issue 43.

Myatt, M. and Thompsett, J. (2022) *Primary Huh: Curriculum Conversations with Subject Leaders in Primary Schools*. Woodbridge: John Catt Educational.

Perry, G. (2016) 'Inside Grayson Perry's sketchbook' on *The Guardian* [online] Available at: www.theguardian.com/artanddesign/2016/feb/19/inside-grayson-perrys-sketchbook (Accessed: 14 May 2026).

CHAPTER 2
DEBATES AND PERSPECTIVES

Art and design in primary schools carries with it many debates and perspectives, with valid arguments on all sides. Those considered in this chapter make for good discussion among practitioners, particularly when reflecting on classroom experiences and the expectations placed on pupils. As noted throughout this book, there is no one-size-fits-all approach to teaching the subject, and there are many ways to deliver it effectively.

What A Good One Looks Like (WAGOLL) versus no WAGOLL

Setting a standard of expectation for pupils is an important part of teaching and learning. Across subjects, many teachers either create in the moment with their class or prepare a What A Good One Looks Like (WAGOLL) beforehand, sharing the key features of a task and giving pupils a concrete model to see. The aim is to ensure pupils understand what's expected and to inspire high-quality outcomes from all. In art and design, WAGOLLs might be sketchbook pages, finished outcomes or stages in a journey to a finished piece, created by the teacher or by pupils from previous year groups.

When used effectively, WAGOLLs have a positive impact on learning. They inspire pupils to work independently, and with a clear understanding of the expectations of a task in hand. They can be particularly useful for those who find the initiation of a task difficult and the blank white space on a page daunting. WAGOLLs not only show an outcome, but they also provide an example from which to discuss starting points.

When selecting or creating a WAGOLL, teachers must carefully consider what they place before pupils. It must set a high standard for the class while remaining realistically achievable. The use of models is firmly rooted in research on effective teaching. One of Barak Rosenshine's (2012) 10 Principles of Instruction is to 'provide models', drawing on cognitive science evidence that worked examples reduce cognitive load and help pupils grasp new techniques. The level at which a model is pitched matters too. Set the bar too high and pupils won't learn from it; set it too low and they won't either. In his blog post 'What should we do with WAGOLLs?' (2023), Alex Quigley calls this the 'Goldilocks principle'. Goldilocks wasn't happy with her porridge being too cold or too hot; she wanted it just right. Pupils need a WAGOLL that is just right too, and teachers have to aim for Baby Bear's porridge.

The downside of a WAGOLL is pupil tendency to copy; to see it as the only route to meeting the objectives and needs of the task set out by the teacher. In art and design, where unique outcomes are encouraged, creativity embraced and individuality celebrated, WAGOLLs can be a disruptor to this notion. Quigley (2023) discusses this with reference to writing, and suggests sharing two examples rather than one for pupils to explore, giving a richer picture of the variety of response possibilities, which is of benefit in art lessons too.

Convergent outcomes versus divergent outcomes

The terms *convergent* and *divergent*, mentioned in the 'Research review series: art and design' (Ofsted, 2023), refer to the categories of curriculum endpoints set by leaders in school. Convergent outcomes are those prescribed by the teacher, as opposed to divergent, where pupils are given more choice. So, which outcomes should teachers provide the learning conditions for in art and design?

Convergent endpoints fit the teaching and learning of specific techniques, where pupils have prescribed exercises to complete to rehearse particular skills such as colour-mixing, drawing and painting techniques. The route to these outcomes is controlled and fixed by the teacher, with all pupils carrying out the same task. Pupils must be taught these skills explicitly and be given ample time to practise them in a quest for mastery.

Divergent outcomes embrace creativity, individuality and difference. Pupils are given choice over their artwork, with exploration and expression at the heart of the activity. They may have ownership of the subject matter they represent in their artwork or the media and tools to create it. A unit of work may focus on portraits, with pupils being introduced to the work of many portrait artists working in different styles, from which they can draw inspiration to create a portrait in their own style.

Example

I'm thinking of a Year 4 unit on printmaking that concludes with each pupil creating their own print inspired by 'The Great Wave off Kanagawa' by Katsushika Hokusai. If it's well planned, this unit has both convergent and divergent sections; it needs both if it's to succeed.

The first lessons are convergent. All pupils learn the same skills: how to roll printing ink to the correct consistency on a tray, how to lower a sheet of paper without disturbing the ink on the block, how to rub with even pressure using the back of a wooden spoon, how to lift the paper without smudging the print. The objectives at the end of these lessons are non-negotiable. Each pupil will have produced a series of test prints using the same simple polystyrene tile, and each pupil's set of prints should look broadly similar when they've finished. The reason for these convergent objectives is simple: pupils cannot express themselves using a technique they've not mastered, and the only evidence of mastery is a print that works.

The final lessons are divergent. Having learned to print, pupils now print something of their own. They've been studying Hokusai's wave as well as many other artistic interpretations of natural forces, including storms by Hiroshige and Turner's turbulent seas, as well as photographs of breaking waves, so the objective now is for pupils to produce their own prints on that theme. The teacher has supplied materials and is available for consultation, but the decisions are now made by the pupils. What force do they want to depict? How do they want to compose it? What colour palette will they use? How will they treat the lines of their image? The end products of these lessons could not be more divergent. One pupil might make a wave, while another draws inspiration from the same theme to print a windswept forest or the swirling smoke from a fire. Compared to one another, their prints should look nothing alike; that is absolutely the point.

The unit works because each mode does what it is required to do. Without the *convergent* stage, there would be no foundation for the divergent work, and pupils would spend their time frustrated, unable to make prints at all. Without the *divergent* stage, the teacher would build skills but miss the opportunity to create a genuinely artistic experience; 30 identical test prints can't hold a candle to what pupils actually create.

You'll find this pattern reproduced in most successfully planned art lessons in primary school. There is a period of teacher-led, convergent work to build technique, followed by a period for pupils to demonstrate what they've learned in an open-ended way. The decision for teachers is not which mode they want to teach in; it's how much of each mode to allocate within a unit.

To answer the question (Which outcomes are best for teachers to work towards with their pupils?): The answer is both; both have a place in the subject of art and design, and suit different areas and objectives of the curriculum.

Nature versus nurture

Have you ever heard teachers make comments along the lines of 'she's naturally gifted' or 'his mum is an art teacher; it's in the genes' when talking about particular pupils in their class? How much truth is in this? Is artistic ability all down to genes or can artists be created? The nature versus nurture debate is a longstanding one and there has been much research relating it to the concept of creativity.

A 2015 study by Velázquez, Segal and Horwitz, published in *Personality and Individual Differences*, set out to assess the contribution of genes and environment to applied creativity. The researchers worked with 69 pairs of identical twins and 53 pairs of fraternal twins from the Minnesota Study of Twins Reared Apart, asking each twin to complete a Draw-a-Person task and a Draw-a-House task. The drawings were assessed by four artists and four non-artists. Velázquez et al. reported genetic effects on the Draw-a-Person task in the range of .38 to .47; no genetic effect on the Draw-a-House task; and a heritability estimate of .50 for creative personality. The authors concluded that both genetic and environmental influences shape applied creativity. Therefore, while some children may have a head start, every child stands to develop as an artist when given strong teaching, deliberate practice and rich experience.

So, nurturing every pupil in art lessons is of utmost importance. Every child can develop, grow and succeed as an artist with the right learning conditions and support. Pupils don't have to be born with it; artistic talent can be taught. Pablo Picasso was right: *every child is an artist.*

Process versus product

What's more important: the process or the product? The answer is both! Like in a maths paper where pupils are asked to show their working out, the process pupils undertake in the creation of their artwork is important and should be celebrated – as should their final outcomes. Observations of children working through the creative process tells a lot about them as artists, and can be used by teachers to help develop next steps for them.

In the world of early years, there is a lot of debate surrounding process versus product art. Many settings follow a 'colour by numbers' approach to expressive arts and design, where pupils are given a step-by-step route to an outcome, guided by a teacher, which looks the same as everyone else's in their class: think paper-plate ladybirds, pop-up spring chickens, handprint dinosaurs with googly eyes, and so on. These are all very lovely activities, with safe, prescribed outcomes, but how do pupils actually benefit from creating them if they are being guided every single step of the way? Well, there are benefits, but they don't support the nurture of creativity; rather, they support the development of fine motor skills and the ability to follow instructions.

▼ **Table 2.1 Process versus product**

Process	Product
• Process art is child initiated • The teacher is there to support if needed, e.g. to aid cutting or sticking or to answer questions about how to do something • It's a creative experience • Outcomes differ • Outcomes may not be wall-worthy art!	• Product art is prescribed by the teacher • It has step-by-step outcomes • The teacher helps pupils 'get it right' • There is a right and a wrong • There is no real variety in outcomes

Process art is where pupils immerse themselves in the experience of the making rather than worrying about outcomes because there is no right or wrong. It's free and open-ended, allowing pupils to express their individuality and make choices. They explore the materials and tools they are making with creatively. Through this process, pupils discover, make links and create using their imaginations. Teachers can provide pupils with a variety of materials and let them play.

Summary

Running through each of these four debates is one simple fact: answers in art and design are very rarely black or white. WAGOLL or no WAGOLL, convergent or divergent, nature or nurture, process or product: the trick is not deciding which is right but knowing how and when to balance the two within a unit, throughout a year or across a whole-school curriculum.

The art teachers who really get it right are the ones who hold both ends of these spectrums in their minds simultaneously, knowing which pupil needs which type of experience at any given moment.

The chapters that follow move beyond these big-picture debates to the nuts and bolts of planning the curriculum itself, starting with what we know from recent research into how primary art and design should be taught.

Further reading

Eisner, E.W. (2002) *The Arts and the Creation of Mind*. New Haven: Yale University Press.

Hetland, L., Winner, E., Veenema, S. and Sheridan, K.M. (2013) *Studio Thinking 2: The Real Benefits of Visual Arts Education*. 2nd edn. New York: Teachers College Press.

Quigley, A. 'What should we do with WAGOLLs?' on Alex Quigley.co.uk [online] Available at: https://alexquigley.co.uk/what-should-we-do-with-wagolls (Accessed: 15 May 2026).

Sherrington, T. and Caviglioli, O. (2020) *Teaching Walkthrus: Five-step Guides to Instructional Coaching*. Woodbridge: John Catt Educational.

Velázquez, J.A., Segal, N.L. and Horwitz, B.N. (2015) 'Genetic and environmental influences on applied creativity: A reared-apart twin study' in *Personality and Individual Differences* 75(5), pp.141–146.

CHAPTER 3
SUBJECT-SPECIFIC RESEARCH

The contents of this book are not only written based on years of experience in the field of primary education but are also informed by contemporary research into the teaching of primary art and design. In this chapter, you will find brief synopses of some important, recent research providing food for thought for primary practitioners. These are only some key headlines from each piece of research; reading each in full is recommended.

Ofsted 'Research review series: art and design' (2023)

Published by Ofsted, this is a review of research into high-quality art and design teaching and learning. Among other aspects of provision in schools, it explores the literature on curriculum progression, pedagogy and assessment in art and design. A key quotation from the report states that art in schools 'at its best should be both intellectually challenging and creatively demanding'.

Knowledge in art can be categorised in a variety of different ways, and much debate ensues when it is discussed. The broadness of the subject requires pupils to develop a knowledge and understanding of skills and techniques linked to media and art forms, artists, history, theory, creative careers, culture and more. The Research Review categorises knowledge in art into three domains: **practical**, **theoretical** and **disciplinary**. Ofsted (2023) acknowledges that researchers in the field have approached this question in different ways. Some have proposed 'foundational art disciplines', covering art production, art history, art criticism and aesthetics. Others have written about productive, critical and cultural domains, or distinguished between learning about, with, in and through art. What unites these accounts is the recognition that art has its own subject-specific forms of knowledge. The Research Review's terminology of practical, theoretical and disciplinary knowledge is offered as a synthesis of these traditions, chosen because it aligns with the aims of the national curriculum for art and design and connects to wider traditions in art education.

Each domain may be focused on in isolation during lessons but, more often than not, and arguably most effectively, they overlap. The areas of knowledge are most meaningful to pupils when woven together purposefully, allowing for connections to be made. A quality art curriculum ensures pupils are provided with experiences that allow not only the introduction of such knowledge, but also frequent opportunities to revisit and retrieve, develop and extend it.

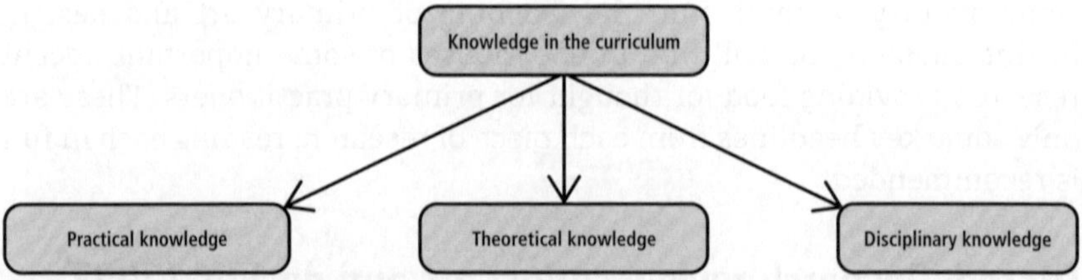

▲ **Figure 3.1 The different strands of knowledge**

Practical knowledge

Practical knowledge refers to the skills linked to the actual *making* part of the *creative* process. The 'knowing how to' make, do, cut, glue, paint, draw, and so on are all part of this domain; those practical skills that equip pupils with a toolkit to function as independent, confident artists. Such skills include knowing how to hold a pencil or paintbrush; knowing sketching techniques such as hatching, cross-hatching or stippling; knowing how to mix certain tints, tones and shades with paint. Over time, pupils should be taught knowledge and skills in methods and techniques for each of the art disciplines (such as drawing, painting and sculpting) to be refined and built upon as they move through school. Each discipline, and its associated media and materials, carries with it a whole set of unique knowledge and skills to be learned and applied. Some skills cross over multiple disciplines and media, while others are more specific and distinct. As well as learning these skills, pupils also need to be able to talk about them using subject-specific vocabulary.

To summarise, practical knowledge encompasses:

- practical skills associated with different art disciplines
- how to use different media, and the artistic capabilities of each
- knowledge and understanding of associated subject-specific vocabulary
- knowledge and understanding of the formal elements of art.

Theoretical knowledge

This domain of knowledge gives pupils the opportunity to put their practical skills and knowledge into context; to make connections between their own practice and that of significant, relevant artists. They learn about art history and its meanings. Pupils need to learn about art's impact on culture, society and the history of the world.

To summarise, theoretical knowledge encompasses:

- knowledge of artists
- knowledge of artworks
- knowledge of the movements in art history.

Disciplinary knowledge

This domain refers to the unique nature of art and its purpose. This knowledge area is where subject-specific connections are made, and a true understanding of the subject is embedded. To acquire disciplinary knowledge, pupils need more than the curriculum on paper; more than prescribed tasks and teacher talk. Disciplinary knowledge takes time to build and is related to the opportunities and experiences pupils are exposed to. Pupils need to learn how to interpret, talk about and appreciate artworks in terms of their stories as well as their techniques and media.

To summarise, disciplinary knowledge encompasses:

- knowledge of the uniqueness of the subject of art
- knowledge of what art is
- knowledge of how to look at and talk about art.

The Ofsted report sets out the pedagogical approaches suited to the teaching and learning of each of these domains of knowledge, which are further explored in Chapter 5.

SEND

It is recognised that there is by no means a one-size-fits-all approach to SEND in the primary art class. Teachers need to have high expectations for all pupils and adapt expectations and processes where necessary to ensure all can succeed.

Imagine a Year 3 class teaching pupils about observational drawing. The whole class are drawing the same still life of autumn leaves, conkers and seed heads. Each pupil has exactly the same learning objective for the lesson: to record what they see in front of them using line, shape and tone. Differentiation is then made around that shared objective. It isn't swapped out for something new. The pupil with a fine-motor difficulty might work on bigger paper with thick graphite sticks instead of a pencil. This removes the challenge of the physical act of drawing. The pupil with a visual impairment may have one leaf sitting on black sugar paper in front of them within easy reach. They may also have the support of a magnifier to help them see it better. The autistic pupil who struggles with open-ended tasks might be given a small card viewfinder to help them focus on one small section of the still life at a time. The pupil with an EHCP for cognition and learning may have the support of a teaching assistant to prompt them to look at the still life, draw what they see, look at the model and repeat the process. The pupils are all doing exactly the same activity: observational drawing. They're all working towards the same learning objective, but the route taken to get there has been tailored to their individual needs.

Assessment

The Ofsted report discusses the need for both formative and summative assessment methods, but recognises the challenges that come from the subjective nature of art. See Chapter 10 for a more detailed discussion of this aspect of primary art and design.

Art-K and YouGov Survey (2025)

In early 2025, the after-school art-education provider art-K commissioned YouGov to survey a nationally representative sample of 569 primary-school teachers about the state of art and design provision in UK primary schools (art-K, 2025). The survey explored teachers' perceptions of fine motor-skill development and the place of art and design on the school timetable. Its key findings were that:

- 77% of teachers had noticed a deterioration in pupils' ability to perform precise movements, such as holding a pencil, drawing, writing or using scissors, since early 2020
- 76% of teachers agreed that quality art and design education is not prioritised in schools
- 18% of teachers reported spending no time teaching art and design in an average week

- 12% of teachers managed to provide more than 60 minutes of art and design education in a week
- 26% of teachers believed pupils were reaching their artistic potential within the current curriculum
- 71% of teachers identified a relationship between art activities, handwriting development and mathematical problem-solving abilities
- 81% of teachers agreed that improving art education would enhance pupil wellbeing
- 21% of teachers believed parents / carers valued art teaching at school.

The RAPS Project: Researching the Arts in Primary Schools (2025)

Researching the Arts in Primary Schools (RAPS) was led by Pat Thomson and Christine Hall with Liam Maloy at the University of Nottingham's School of Education. Funded by the Freelands Foundation, the research aimed to explore primary schools where the arts and creative practice are flourishing. Thomson, Hall and Maloy (2025) undertook a survey of 76 primary schools deemed to be doing well in arts and creative practice, identifying 40 schools for in-depth case-study work and 22 schools to act as comparators against the schools included in the Education Endowment Foundation (EEF) family of schools dataset. This gave answers to four research questions:

- What is an arts-rich primary school?
- What do arts-rich and creative primary schools offer to children?
- What are the benefits to children of being in an arts-rich or creative school?
- How do schools sustain this arts and creative education offer?

Methods used included:

- a survey of arts-rich schools (n=76)
- interviews with pupils (n=854) and adults (n=150) (primarily teachers and senior leaders)
- a classroom-teacher survey, which returned 151 responses from 16 schools
- a Year 5 pupil survey, which returned 1017 responses
- documentary and photographic evidence collected from 41 schools

- school-level data from the 76 schools
- comparator performance data from the 22 RAPS schools and 44 EEF family schools.

The key findings from the research make a compelling argument for the arts in the primary curriculum. Committing to arts and creative practice has sustained benefits for pupil engagement and attainment, and this does not come at the cost of other subjects. So, if you're a school leader thinking about prioritising the arts but concerned about your performance data in core subjects, the RAPS research has an answer for you: it doesn't negatively impact performance in core subjects (Thomson, Hall and Maloy, 2025).

The 'Visualise' report (2024)

'Visualise: Race and Inclusion in Secondary School Art Education', published by the Runnymede Trust and Freelands Foundation in 2024, was the first large-scale study into race and ethnicity in art education in England. The report's authors spoke to pupils, artists, teachers and others, who described art as a unique space in the curriculum: a place where pupils are invited to respond to the world around them and reflect on their own place within it. Inclusion in the art classroom, then, is not a 'bolt-on'. It is integral to what art education should strive to achieve.

Secondary art

The report makes for uncomfortable reading. It demonstrates that, of named artists featured in GCSE Art exam papers, only 1.54% are identified as being from a black background and 0.74% as South Asian, giving a total of just 2.3% of artists from marginalised ethnic groups (Runnymede Trust and Freelands Foundation, 2024). Attitudes among pupils suggest that they understand the importance of this statistic: two-thirds of those questioned wanted to study art by a diverse range of artists, rising to 80% of black pupils. Teachers expressed a lack of confidence in teaching artists from outside the established canon for fear of using inappropriate language, and they also cited a shortage of supporting resources.

Primary art

The report focused on race and ethnicity in secondary arts provision. But what does this data look like through primary lenses? How diverse is the curriculum being studied? What resources are read? Do teachers have confidence teaching about art and artists from diverse backgrounds?

Windows and mirrors

'Visualise' drew on the windows-and-mirrors metaphor offered by Emily Style in her 1988 essay 'Curriculum as Window and Mirror'. Style argued that pupils should be taught with both mirrors and windows: a curriculum that functions as a window opens onto the lives, experiences and realities of others, while one that functions as a mirror reflects pupils' own identities back to them. Teaching art and artists from a range of styles, techniques and cultures does more than diversify the statistics; it ensures that every pupil can identify with the art they are studying.

Mirrors are in short supply, according to 'Visualise', but they can be sourced. Pupils in every setting are entitled to a diet of artists as rich and varied as their interests and capacities. Long-celebrated white European male artists have their place; no canon should be discarded wholesale. But when planning a curriculum, teachers should think beyond Monet, Picasso and Van Gogh. Diversity of race, ethnicity and identity is not simply a box to be ticked. Teachers should ask themselves who is depicted on their classroom walls, whose art is celebrated and whose stories are told. Pupils should be able to see themselves there. As Keith Piper writes in the foreword to 'Visualise', the work ahead is one of seeking out new artists and overlooked stories and creating the resources teachers need to teach them confidently.

Every pupil has a right to see themselves in the curriculum; a right to feel that they can achieve; a right to relate to what is in front of them; a right to feel that they belong. This is regardless of race, sex, age, religion or disability. The art curriculum in a school needs to be tailored to suit the unique demographic of its community. A carefully curated selection of artist studies and art-appreciation foci ensures all pupils feel a sense of belonging, inspiration to succeed and a drive to believe they can. This helps them feel connected to the curriculum, interested and more likely to develop a deeper understanding of the concepts they study. The 'mirrors' that Emily Style referred to play an invaluable role in a child's feelings of self-worth through the provision of positive reflections of themselves. With this in mind, it is essential that art leaders and class teachers know their school community well.

> Growing up, I didn't see myself reflected in the artists we studied at school. The names, the faces, the stories – they felt distant. There were no artists who looked like me, none whose journeys resonated with my own lived experience. Art felt like something

that belonged to another world – a world I could admire but not fully enter – which is why drawing became so personal to me.

No one came into our classrooms who could bridge that gap. There were no visiting artists who looked like they came from my community, no one to stand at the front of the room and say, 'You can do this too.' As a young boy who loved to draw, it sometimes felt like I was moving through a system that hadn't made space for someone like me.

And yet, that absence pushed me to create my own path. It became fuel. I wanted to draw so precisely, so honestly, that the world would have to look back and see – see me, see the people I draw, see our stories with the same reverence given to those long upheld in art history books.

Representation isn't just important. It's powerful. It tells us that we exist, that our creativity matters. And now, through my work, I hope to be the presence I never had growing up – the artist a young person might see and think, 'That could be me.'

Kelvin Okafor, Artist
www.kelvinokaforart.com

Teachers need to value and empathise with their pupils; pupils need to feel like they all matter. Communicating with pupils, listening to them and taking an interest in their lives is key. Only then can those designing learning be sure that the curriculum they are offering is reflecting the whole class or school body. This is an important step in providing an inclusive, equitable and personalised art curriculum. Even if using published schemes, ensure they are tailored to a school setting by including artists and art from the community. That way, the scheme will fit perfectly with the cohort of pupils being taught.

As well as providing mirrors, we need to ensure our art curriculums provide windows: opportunities for pupils to look out into the world and learn about other people's experiences. If all that pupils see are mirrors in their lessons, they will have a limited understanding of the broader human experience. They won't develop empathy for others or an accurate worldview. One of the goals of a well-rounded education is to help create global citizens; citizens who understand and value difference. Art education in the primary classroom can play a significant role in helping pupils to achieve that aim.

Style (1988) explains how, if we educate pupils in a vacuum and teach them only about their immediate surroundings, we fail to equip them for the global world they will grow up in. Pupils need windows and mirrors, and they need to see many different examples of each to develop a healthy understanding of where they fit in the world.

School art curricula differ from town to town, school to school and, quite often, between classrooms in the same school. Artists and artworks should be selected thoughtfully and intentionally to reflect the community the school serves. One school's mirror might be another school's window. As Marie C. Wilson (2007) put it, 'you can't be what you can't see'. Pupils need to see that people who look like them have platforms as artists. They need to know that art, craft and design is for everyone.

Further reading

Art-K / YouGov (2025) 'A new YouGov survey commissioned by art-K reveals that there's a crisis in creative learning' [online] Available at: www.art-k.co.uk/art-education-neglected (Accessed: 15 May 2026).

Begum, Dr S., Wylie, M., Anwari, H. and Hood, S. (2024) 'Visualise: Race and Inclusion in Secondary School Art Education' by the Runnymede Trust and Freelands Foundation [online] Available at: www.runnymedetrust.org/publications/visualise-race-and-inclusion-in-secondary-school-art-education (Accessed: 15 May 2026).

Bishop, R.S. (1990) 'Mirrors, windows, and sliding glass doors' in *Perspectives*, 6(3), pp.ix–xi.

National Society for Education in Art and Design (NSEAD) 'Anti-Racist Art Education Action Resources'. Corsham: NSEAD. [online] Available at: www.nsead.org/resources/anti-racist-art-education (Accessed: 15 May 2026).

Ofsted (2023) 'Research review series: art and design' [online] Available at: www.gov.uk/government/publications/research-review-series-art-and-design (Accessed: 14 May 2026).

Thomson, P. Hall, C. and Maloy, L. (2025) *The RAPS Project: Researching the Arts in Primary Schools*, University of Nottingham and Freelands Foundation [online] Available at: https://artsprimary.com/wp-content/uploads/2025/02/raps-final-feb-2025--4.pdf (Accessed: 27 July 2026).

CHAPTER 4
AGE PROGRESSION

The 2024 'Manifesto' of the National Society for Education in Art and Design (NSEAD) makes a call for pupils across all education stages and settings to be in receipt of a 'learner-centred, future-facing contemporary curriculum' with an 'equity of opportunity for all'. Pupils need a curriculum that supports the development of confidence and curiosity and provides meaningful and purposeful connections. In the primary setting, this, alongside a sprinkling of excitement and magic, helps make the art classroom a place where pupils want and long to be, and if they want and long to be somewhere, they're more likely to listen, absorb, develop and grow.

An ambitious primary school art and design curriculum is one that:

- at least meets the requirements of the national curriculum
- develops practical, theoretical and disciplinary subject knowledge
- provides opportunity for progression through clear sequences of learning
- is diverse and inclusive
- is broad and balanced
- is rooted in context and community
- provides both mirrors and windows for pupils.

Whether creating an art and design curriculum from scratch, or choosing one off the shelf, schools should carefully consider a number of factors when curating their subject provision. The curriculum needs to encompass, encourage and facilitate high expectations, optimum progress and quality outcomes for all. Its content and delivery methods need to be diverse and inclusive, with all pupils taking part in supportive learning experiences that provide pathways to success. Art and design curricula need to be broad and balanced, exciting pupils through carefully curated blends of art disciplines, media, tools and techniques. All this should be illustrated and meaningfully connected through artist studies; opportunities to compare, contrast and talk; and set in the context of both the contemporary world and times gone by.

It is important, however, that schools, in their quest to provide a broad scope of knowledge and experiences, do not fall into the trap of delivering a curriculum that is too wide-ranging. Trying to fit too much in can lead to superficial, surface-level learning, with pupils not having the opportunity to progress and master what they are taught. As Myatt (2020) put it, the answer is fewer things in greater depth.

Before looking specifically at granular steps of progression in the subject, this chapter tackles the statements for art and design within the national curriculum one at a time. It is with a true understanding of these statements that school leaders and curriculum shapers can begin to focus on the small steps of progression that pupils may take, and plan out intentional learning experiences to develop and nurture them.

The national curriculum

The national curriculum subject descriptors for primary art and design are short and brief: a mere four statements for key stage 1 and only three for key stage 2:

> **Key stage 1**
>
> Pupils should be taught:
>
> - to use a range of materials creatively to design and make products
> - to use drawing, painting and sculpture to develop and share their ideas, experiences and imagination
> - to develop a wide range of art and design techniques in using colour, pattern, texture, line, shape, form and space
> - about the work of a range of artists, craft makers and designers, describing the differences and similarities between different practices and disciplines, and making links to their own work.
>
> **Key stage 2**
>
> Pupils should be taught to develop their techniques, including their control and their use of materials, with creativity, experimentation and an increasing awareness of different kinds of art, craft and design.
>
> Pupils should be taught:
>
> - to create sketchbooks to record their observations and use them to review and revisit ideas

- to improve their mastery of art and design techniques, including drawing, painting and sculpture with a range of materials [for example, pencil, charcoal, paint, clay]
- about great artists, architects and designers in history.

(DfE, 2013)

Consequently, educators are provided with just the bare bones on which to build art provisions for their schools. This can be either a blessing or a struggle, depending on school context: a blessing for schools with a skilled, confident art lead who can enthusiastically use the statements as a base to develop a broad, balanced, exciting and ambitious creative curriculum; a struggle for those without in-house subject specialists, for whom the lack of detail in expectations can make curriculum building a tricky task.

Key stage 1

So, let's unpick those national curriculum content headlines, starting with KS1: What do they mean and what might they look like in practice?

Pupils should be taught to use a range of materials creatively to design and make products

This first descriptor is somewhat self-explanatory, covering the practical knowledge associated with using different materials and tools to create artwork, the 'materials' in this statement being the elements, the component parts, that pupils use to create and piece their work together.

So, when thinking about drawing, for example, the materials used could be pencils, pens, charcoal, pastels or chalks, among other mark-making tools, which can be used to make marks on paper, walls, canvases, fabrics, and more. In a similar vein, painting experiences do not need to be limited to the ready-mixed poster paint found in many a store cupboard. Pupils love and benefit from exploring and investigating the capabilities of different paint types: watercolours, acrylics, powder paint or even paints made from the natural world or kitchen cupboards. These paints can be used with a variety of different brushes, ranging from fine art to decorator size. Brushes can also be made from objects found either in the classroom, such as scrunched-up paper, or the great outdoors, such as leaves and sticks – the possibilities really are endless!

The aim of this statement is to ensure pupils receive an engaging, inspiring and varied curriculum; one that opens pupils' eyes to the extensive open-ended possibilities the subject can lead them to. Here, we are thinking about both the designing and making aspects of the creative process, so it's important that schools allow pupils the opportunity to think, plan, try out and think again, before they start their making.

Notice how the descriptor states that pupils need to be taught how to use the materials. So, it is important that teachers model and demonstrate different skills and techniques associated with each, as well as giving pupils the chance to play and explore for themselves. Table 4.1 gives a list of materials that could be used within each of the main primary-school art disciplines mentioned in the national curriculum. This list is by no means exhaustive, but is a great starting point.

▼ **Table 4.1 Materials for each of the primary-school art disciplines**

Art discipline	Possible materials to use
Drawing	• graphite pencils • sketching pencils • charcoal • chalk • pens • crayons • wool / string • oil pastels
Painting	• watercolour paint • acrylic paint • powder paint • ink • mud • fruit juices • blended greens such as spinach • tea / coffee
Sculpting	• clay • play dough • paper • foil • cardboard • wire • soap

Pupils should be taught to use drawing, painting and sculpture to develop and share their ideas, experiences and imagination

Here, the need for pupils to create art in different ways and for differing purposes is outlined. So, rather than experience an art diet solely of drawing from imagination, painting with watercolours and reproducing carbon copies of the work of famous artists throughout their primary schooling, pupils should be exposed to a variety of experiences and sequences of learning. They should *at least* be taught to draw, paint and sculpt to share their ideas, experiences and imagination.

Pupils should be taught to develop a wide range of art and design techniques in using colour, pattern, texture, line, shape, form and space

This descriptor outlines the need for pupils to develop an understanding of the formal elements of art, which it lists for ease and understanding. It's useful to think of these elements as the building blocks of art. They are the components artists use when creating artwork.

Pupils should be taught about the work of a range of artists, craft makers and designers, describing the differences and similarities between different practices and disciplines, and making links to their own work

Another pretty self-explanatory statement, but one that perhaps needs picking apart carefully.

Firstly, the word 'taught': What do we need to teach pupils about these artists? We need to think about their place in art history, their styles, techniques and subjects. We need to think about how their work can engage and inspire our pupils to become better educated and aware as artists.

The next word of extreme importance here is 'range'. We need to ensure pupils encounter a wide variety of artists across difference times, spaces and places. It's also worth noting that the national curriculum doesn't mention only artists, but craft makers and designers too. Over time, pupils should develop a bank of knowledge about the creatives they have been introduced to and should know and understand how to talk about art, comparing the similarities and differences between the artistic processes and artwork of artists, including themselves.

Key stage 2

Now, let's do the same with KS2.

Pupils should be taught to create sketchbooks to record their observations to review and revisit ideas

This statement appears only as a KS2 requirement, but many schools choose to begin using sketchbooks at KS1. These books are different from other exercise books used in classrooms, not only in the content that goes in them, but also in style and teacher-feedback contributions too. The development of sketchbook use takes time, and the earlier pupils begin developing this habit and understanding, the better.

Despite their name, 'sketchbooks' aren't just for sketching in, but for exploring all kinds of media and techniques; for rehearsing and refining skills; recording research, thoughts, feelings, annotations; and more. Sketchbooks are for recording complete art and design learning journeys, and places that show progression and evidence of thinking and working like an artist.

Pupils should be taught to improve their mastery of art and design techniques, including drawing, painting and sculpture with a range of materials [for example, pencil, charcoal, paint, clay]

Throughout their KS2 journey, pupils continue to progress as artists, refining, developing and adding to the skills and knowledge introduced to them at KS1. This descriptor suggests they should be 'taught' to improve; this can be taught by the teacher or by themselves through discovery and exploration. A high-quality art curriculum provides opportunities for both.

Many schools, as well as drawing, painting and sculpture, also select one or more additional areas of making to inspire their pupils (note the descriptor says 'including drawing, painting and sculpture', which suggests other areas are not just permitted but actively expected). The National Society for Education in Art and Design (NSEAD) outlines 12 areas of making: drawing, painting, printmaking, sculpture, ceramics, creative craft, collage, textiles, photography, installation, digital media and design. The areas a school chooses to focus on will depend on its unique context, including its staff skillset, school facilities, local area and traditions.

Pupils should be taught about great artists, architects and designers in history

This statement is an extension of the final KS1 descriptor. The national curriculum writers have added in the word 'great', but that serves no real purpose: How do we define a 'great' artist, architect or designer? The individuals we inspire our pupils with need to be *relevant*; they don't even need to be *famous*.

It's important to note the addition of the world of architecture onto the curriculum in KS2.

Progression of skills

With an understanding of the national curriculum descriptors for KS1 and KS2, alongside an awareness of the knowledge domains in the subject, school and subject leaders can construct a model of progression for pupils in their school. It's important to consider that progression in art and design is not as straightforward as in other subjects on the curriculum, the end goals being the drivers shaping any preceding small steps of learning.

These end goals can vary from setting to setting, depending on context and chosen curriculum foci. Ultimately, however, a school's aim is for their pupils to know more, remember more and increase their mastery of artistic skills as they journey through their years of primary education. To do this, curriculum designers need to ensure that consistent threads and progressive steps exist from Early Years Foundation Stage (EYFS) to Year 6.

The comprehensive progression map shown in Table 4.2 was created by Mandy Barrett, artist and art-specialist teacher at Gomersal Primary School in West Yorkshire, a school well known for its high-quality teaching and learning, expertise in the subject and generous sharing of resources on its art blog 'Gomersal Primary School Art'. Mandy's progression documentation provides an ambitious benchmark for proficiencies and understanding in primary art and design from Year 1 through to Year 6. EYFS experiences prepare pupils for the expectations of the KS1 national curriculum.

The following suggested expectations of an EYFS pupil would feed into the progression map:

Drawing – an EYFS artist will:

- hold a pencil
- draw controlled lines and use the skill to make different shapes
- interpret an object through drawing
- express feelings through drawing.

Painting – an EYFS artist will:

- experiment with a range of painting equipment
- paint controlled lines and use the skill to make different shapes
- mix colours
- describe how the mixed colours have changed.

Sculpture – an EYFS artist will:

- use play dough
- use a rolling pin to roll play dough and cut out shapes using cutters
- make marks and textures in the play dough using special rolling pins and everyday objects.

Printing – an EYFS artist will:

- use different tools through printing to create marks
- repeat a print to make a simple pattern
- create a simple pattern.

▼ **Table 4.2 Gomersal Primary School progression of experiences in art, craft and design**

Drawing
A Year 1 Artist will:
• Explore a range of drawing tools to make marks
• Begin to control the types of marks made with a range of media
• Draw on different surfaces
• Explore different textures
• Draw from imagination
• Explore drawing from observation
• Investigate textures by describing, naming, rubbing and copying
• Produce a range of patterns and textures
A Year 2 Artist will:
• Experiment with tools and surfaces
• Draw experiences and feelings
• Sketch to make records
• Begin to control marks made with different media
• Investigate tone by drawing light / dark lines using pencil
• Investigate textures and produce an expanding range of patterns
A Year 3 Artist will:
• Experiment with various pencils
• Use a sketchbook to document and develop ideas
• Draw from observation and imagination
• Experiment with mark-making using alternative tools
• Create initial sketches for painting
• Begin to draw with accuracy
• Discuss shadows, light and dark
• Have an awareness of how pattern can be used to create texture
A Year 4 Artist will:
• Consider scale and proportion
• Create accurate observational drawings
• Work on a variety of scales
• Produce drawings using IT

Drawing

- Identify and draw the effect of light
- Draw for a sustained period of time
- Develop techniques to create intricate patterns – range of media

A Year 5 Artist will:

- Work in a sustained and independent way to create an accurate, detailed drawing, developing key elements of their work (line, tone, pattern, texture)
- Draw from different viewpoints considering horizon lines
- Begin to consider perspective
- Use different techniques for purpose, e.g. different styles of shading
- Work from a variety of sources including observation and photographs to develop own work

A Year 6 Artist will:

- Select appropriate media and techniques to achieve a specific outcome
- Develop their own style
- Draw for a sustained period of time over a number of sessions
- Use tone in drawings to achieve depth
- Develop drawing with perspective and focal points
- Adapt drawings according to evaluations and discuss further developments

Painting

A Year 1 Artist will:

- Begin to explore and experiment with the primary colours
- Mix primary colours to create secondary colours
- Describe collections of colours
- Discuss and use warm and cold colours
- Describe favourite colours and why colours may be used for different purposes
- Explore a range of paint, brush sizes and tools

A Year 2 Artist will:

- Begin to describe a range of colours
- Mix a range of secondary colours
- Talk about why they have selected colours for their artwork
- Begin to use a range of paint

Painting

A Year 3 Artist will:

- Lighten a colour by adding white
- Darken / lighten colours without using black / white (e.g. dilute with water)
- Explore a variety of media to create colour (paint, crayon, coloured pencil, textiles, ink, pastels, etc.)
- Demonstrate increasing control of the types of marks made to create certain effects using paint

A Year 4 Artist will:

- Begin to alter paint colour using white, grey and black
- Observe colour and suggest why it has been used
- Select colour to reflect mood
- Explore different brush strokes and consider why / when they might be used
- Begin to discuss how they are influenced by the work of other artists

A Year 5 Artist will:

- Mix colours with confidence, building on previous knowledge
- Select colour for purpose, explaining choices
- Discuss how colour can be used to express ideas, feelings and mood
- Confidently control the types of marks made and experiment with different effects and textures

A Year 6 Artist will:

- Select colour to express feelings
- Work in a sustained and independent way, developing own style
- Purposefully control the types of marks / brushstrokes used to create desired effect
- Use colours and brushstrokes to create atmosphere and light effects

Sculpture 3D Shape & Form Architecture
A Year 1 Artist will: • Enjoy handling, feeling and manipulating a range of materials • Construct using a range of media • Cut shapes using scissors and other modelling tools in a safe way • Build a construction using a variety of objects • Discuss the different types of buildings in their locality **A Year 2 Artist will:** • Show an awareness that natural and human-made materials can be used to create sculpture • Create models from imagination and direct observation • Join materials together and apply decorative techniques • Discuss the work of other sculptors and relate these to their own ideas and designs **A Year 3 Artist will:** • Plan, shape, mould and make constructions from different materials • Show an awareness of how texture, form and shape can be transferred from 2D to 3D • Demonstrate awareness in environmental sculpture **A Year 4 Artist will:** • Discuss the work of other sculptors and architects and how these have influenced their own work / designs • Make slip to join and secure pieces of clay together • Produce more intricate surface patterns using a range of processes • Adapt work when necessary and explain why **A Year 5 Artist will:** • Develop an understanding of different ways of finishing work (e.g. glaze, paint, varnish) • Understand that a range of media can be selected (due to their properties) for different purposes

Sculpture

- Independently recognise problems and adapt work when necessary – taking inspiration from other sculptors

A Year 6 Artist will:

- Recognise sculptural forms in the environment and use these as inspiration for their own work
- Demonstrate experience in relief and freestanding work using a range of media
- Independently select sculpture as a method of producing work, if this fits the criteria of the task

Printing

A Year 1 Artist will:

- Take rubbings from textured surfaces, e.g. leaf, coin, tree bark
- Print pictures with a range of materials, e.g. sponge, reels
- Begin to explore impressed printing, e.g. with Styrofoam
- Begin to identify different forms of printing, e.g. books, newspapers, fabric, wallpaper

A Year 2 Artist will:

- Explore repeated printing using a range of simple methods
- Explore mono printing
- Identify a wider range of printed forms in everyday life and consider how the processes have changed over time

A Year 3 Artist will:

- Design and create a repeated relief print considering background paper
- Use sketchbooks to explore and develop prints making changes where needed
- Understand the difference between repeat printing and mono printing

A Year 4 Artist will:

- Explore the process of mono printing
- Demonstrate an awareness of printing with multiple colours
- Demonstrate an awareness of printing onto fabric and consider the difference to printing onto paper

Printing
A Year 5 Artist will:
• Gain experience in overlaying colours
• Start to overlay prints with other media
• Continue to experience combining prints to produce an end piece
• Explore, experiment, plan and collect source material for future work
A Year 6 Artist will:
• Use Thermofax screens to explore screen printing
• Combine different printing techniques within the same piece of artwork
• Use print as a starting point to embroidery

Curriculum case studies

Once a provision map has been created, schools can begin to build their art and design curriculums. Here, three schools tell their inspiring stories.

Curriculum case study 1: a curriculum inspired by books

Karl Duke, Headteacher and Headreader at Blyton cum Laughton Church of England Primary School, Lincolnshire

Context

We call the curriculum at Blyton cum Laughton Church of England Primary School the Reading-Inspired Curriculum due to the majority of learning being *inspired* by the high-quality texts we explore; books are our key driver. These texts provide the knowledge and inspire the skills our pupils need. This is no different from many schools, but it was a change we needed to make to guarantee pupils have the opportunity to immerse themselves in books throughout their journey with us. In fact, by the time pupils have completed that journey, they will have explored over 350 books across the majority of subjects, not including those read personally, in worship or through teacher choice.

Before we established our curriculum, pupils generally had little interest in reading and did not appreciate the joy reading can bring. The reading-inspired version of the curriculum has changed our pupils' perspective of what a book can offer and helped create a reading culture. Every term, pupils explore a key book, one that provides a link to the history, geography or science focus, alongside a carefully selected group of supporting books, which aim to deepen understanding and immerse pupils in their learning. These books are a combination of chapter books, picture books, non-fiction texts, graphic novels and poetry. The variety is vital.

Rationale

Our belief: Every child is an artist, and they should be given the guidance and time to let their skills flourish.

During the curriculum-writing process, art was a key subject in providing examples of how books could *deliver* the required knowledge, models and skills. The national curriculum rightly suggests a colourful palette of historically significant artists, but we also chose to balance this focus with the undeniable quality and inspiration of non-fiction and picture-book creators and their respective illustrative styles and techniques. The use of high-quality books to support the teaching of art is an integral part of the change in our reading culture, the improved teacher confidence in delivery and the significant improvement in artistic outcomes.

Alongside famous artists such as Claude Monet, Yayoi Kusama and Edward-Saidi Tingatinga, we are proud to value and take inspiration from illustrators and artists such as Shaun Tan, Jackie Morris and Ben Rothery, as well as picture-book creators including Benjamin Flouw and Sophie Blackall.

Books provide added knowledge and links to wider areas of the curriculum and excellent models for writing; this ensures opportunities for further immersion and immediate examples for teachers to use. Why look elsewhere, when the models are there within the books we are using? For example, Ben Rothery's *Deadly and Dangerous Animals* not only delivers artwork of an exceptional quality – pupils have loved focusing on the clouded leopard section – but the challenging and informative texts are certainly appropriate for KS2 primary-aged pupils.

The development of our art curriculum would not have been possible without the influence of Sophie Merrill's blogs about the use of sketchbooks in primary school. Thanks to Sophie's generosity, we have transformed how we teach art by introducing the use of sketchbooks to explore the work of artists, to experiment with techniques and to build every pupil's confidence in their own skills. Sketchbooks have truly revolutionised our practice and they have had a significant impact on outcomes alongside the emphasis on the teacher modelling every stage through our own sketchbooks or when completing our own finished piece.

Lighthouse work

Each term, pupils are guided into their learning through a class text. For instance, in the Spring Term of Years 5 and 6, the class book is Emma Carroll's *Letters from the Lighthouse*, which is set during World War II. This text is supported by *The Harmonica* by Tony Johnston and Ron Mazellan; *How Does a Lighthouse Work?* by Roman Belyaev; *Rose Blanche* by Christophe Gallaz and Roberto Innocenti; *Erika's Story* by Ruth Zee and Roberto Innocenti; and *Hello, Lighthouse* by Sophie Blackall. The books are used across the curriculum, occasionally fleetingly, often in depth, but all help to paint the picture of learning.

Our aim was always to include picture books throughout the entirety of the curriculum, from EYFS to Year 6. Picture books are accessible to all; a stepping stone to every pupil's learning thanks to the quality of visuals and language, and they help the reader dive into sometimes difficult subject matter at an appropriate level, like *Erika's Story*, for instance. A text such as Sophie Blackall's *Hello, Lighthouse* is a superb example of a book providing background knowledge to support the class text, and one that has helped transform our teaching of art.

By the time pupils reach Upper KS2, they have experienced a range of media and techniques. So, for our *Hello, Lighthouse*-inspired artwork, pupils have the opportunity to develop their pencil drawing (both sketching and coloured), painting and collage skills in a large-scale mixed-media piece. Blackall's cross-section illustration of the lighthouse provides the inspiration.

First, pupils sketch out (on A3 to A2 cartridge paper) the outline of the lighthouse, the rock formation and the horizon line where the sky meets the sea. We always emphasise the importance of getting the proportions of any sketch right first; pupils have developed more patience when doing so and their accuracy has improved.

Then we explore skies that have been painted or photographed so that pupils have the opportunity to experiment with colour and decide on the 'mood' of their piece. Across the group, we always have a range, from stormy through dawn and dusk to the warmth of a summer's day; the discussions around the choice of colour to represent each mood is invaluable. After experimenting with mood colours in their sketchbooks, pupils paint skies using watercolours and a large brush, often settling on a stripe technique to blend the colours as they move from the highest point of the sky to the horizon line.

The next step is to create the coloured-pencil drawings for each floor of the cross-sectioned lighthouse, including the light room. Pupils have always enjoyed playing with the detail required and, with careful modelling, more mature blending techniques can be explored to show progression from their previous work. Time and patience are needed here, as the lighthouse's rooms provide the focal point for the finished piece and provide a contrast to the large-scale brush strokes and collage rocks that surround the lighthouse. The focus is also on colour matching, an area we come back to frequently in our art curriculum.

Before adding the coloured-pencil work to the lighthouse, pupils research the different paint designs of lighthouses and, again, choose their own, often going for the traditional red-and-white stripe design. After painting the lighthouse, the pencil work is glued on accurately, with a proportionate distance between each floor. We talk about 'reference' throughout the process; the reference of Blackall's lighthouse is always at hand to support the young artists. Finer details of the lighthouse are added at the end, but first pupils use paint and textured papers to create the rocks on which the lighthouse stands. The aim of this is for pupils to experiment with tone, being confident to create rocks in a range of colours but with the same tonal feel.

The waves are created after looking at the paintings of Hokusai and the technique used by Sophie Blackall. Their inspiration, particularly the painting of the ocean foam, requires detailed brushwork with the smallest brush and, again, is a contrast to the scale of the collage rocks and sky brush strokes. Less detail is needed as the waves vanish into the distance and the horizontal stripe-brush technique is again deployed to blend waves into the sky. Pupils are encouraged to mirror the colours of the sky in the waves, giving the impression of reflection.

The final task is to add the details to the lighthouse and its surroundings. Pupils may choose to add pipework, ladders, railings, a weathervane and seagulls flying around using paint, pencil or fine-liner pen. Others have created a message in a bottle resting on the rocks – with a real miniature note linked to *Letters from the Lighthouse* – or a rowing boat hanging from the building waiting to be used. These final details bring the whole piece together and add more individuality to the art.

Time to be an artist

Our main philosophy when teaching art is that pupils are given the time to complete a piece of which they can be proud. Time, modelling and quality references – often the books we use – provide pupils with the very best opportunity to display their skills. We strongly believe that outcome quality is at risk of being diminished significantly if less time is available, and this can ultimately make the difference between a pupil believing they are an artist... or not. The incredible gallery of lighthouses, by every pupil, framed and on display in school, are testament to our reading-inspired approach.

Table 4.3 Blyton cum Laughton Church of England Primary School curriculum foci

Term	Inspirational books	Extraordinary lives: artists	Art focus
EYFS			
Autumn Term	• *Action Jackson* by Jan Greenberg & Sandra Jordan • *Yayoi Kusama Covered Everything in Dots and Wasn't Sorry* by Fausto Gilberti	• Jackson Pollock • Yayoi Kusama • Piet Mondrian	• Mark making / drawing • Painting / colour • Printing • 3D work
Spring Term	• *Mixed* by Arree Chung • *The Hungry Caterpillar* by Eric Carle • *Luna Loves Art* by Joseph Coelho & Fiona Lumbers	• Yves Klein • Joan Miró • Andy Goldsworthy • Eric Carle	• Mark making / drawing • Painting / colour • Printing • 3D work • Textiles
Summer Term	• *Katie and the Starry Night* by James Mayhew • *Henri's Scissors* by Jeanette Winter • *Matisse's Magical Trail* by Tim Hopgood & Sam Boughton	• Vincent Van Gogh • Henri Matisse	• Mark making / drawing • Painting / colour • Printing • 3D work • Textiles
Year 1/2			
Cycle 1 Autumn Term	• *We're All Wonders* by R.J. Palacio		• Drawing

Term	Inspirational books	Extraordinary lives: artists	Art focus
Cycle 1 Spring Term	• *Life Size: Spots and Stripes* by Sophie Henn • *The Dreaming Giant: Wassily Kandinsky* by Véronique Massenot & Peggy Nile	• Sophie Henn • Wassily Kandinsky	• Painting
Cycle 1 Summer Term	• *The Mystery of the Golden Wonderflower* by Benjamin Flouw • *The Dinosaurs of Waterhouse Hawkins* by Barbara Kerley and Brian Selznick	• Benjamin Flouw • Megan Coyle • Andy Goldsworthy • Waterhouse Hawkins	• Printing • Sculpture
Cycle 2 Autumn Term	• *The Great Fire of London: Anniversary edition of The Great Fire of 1666* by Emma Adams & James Weston Lewis • *Meerkat Mail* by Emily Gravett	• Kurt Schwitters • Pablo Picasso	• Painting and collage • 3D model-making: masks
Cycle 2 Spring Term	• *The Tin Forest* by Helen Ward & Wayne Anderson • *The Adventures of Robin Hood* by Marcia Williams	• Henry Bradbury • Alois Auer • Andy Goldsworthy	• Printing
Cycle 2 Summer Term	• *The Lost Words* by Robert MacFarlane & Jackie Morris • *What Mr Darwin Saw* by Mick Manning & Brita Granstrom • *Child of St Kilda* by Beth Waters	• Jackie Morris • Beth Waters	• Drawing / painting • Textiles

Term	Inspirational books	Extraordinary lives: artists	Art focus
Year 3/4			
Cycle 1 Autumn Term	• *The First Drawing* by Mordicai Berstein • *Ancestory: The Mystery and Majesty of Ancient Cave Art* by Hannah Salyer • *When We Became Humans* by Michael Bright & Hannah Bailey	• Cave painting	• Drawing and painting
Cycle 1 Spring Term	• *100 Facts: Roman Britain* by Miles Kelly		• Sculpture: jewellery
Cycle 1 Summer Term	• *How to Train Your Dragon* by Cressida Cowell		• 3D model-making: clay
Cycle 2 Autumn Term	• *Everest* by Alexandra Stewart & Joe Todd-Stanton • *Deadly and Dangerous Animals / Hidden Planet* by Ben Rothery	• Katsushika Hokusai • Ben Rothery	• Drawing and painting
Cycle 2 Spring Term	• *A River* by Marc Martin • *Portrait of an Artist: Claude Monet* by Lucy Brownridge & Caroline Bonne Müller	• Claude Monet	• Painting and collage
Cycle 2 Summer Term	• *Found: Anglo-Saxon Britain* by Moira Butterfield		• Textiles
Year 4/5			
Cycle 1 Autumn Term	• *The Invention of Hugo Cabret* by Brian Selznick	• Brian Selznick	• Drawing

Term	Inspirational books	Extraordinary lives: artists	Art focus
Cycle 1 Spring Term	• *The Big Book of Blue* by Yuval Zommer	• Yuval Zommer • Olga Nikitina	• Painting
Cycle 1 Summer Term	• *Wild Animals of the South* by Dieter Braun	• Daudi Tingatinga	• Printing
Cycle 2 Autumn Term	• *Outlaw* by Michael Morpurgo • *Discovering Heraldry* by Jacqueline Fearn		• Drawing and painting
Cycle 2 Summer Term	• *Rain Player* by David Wisniewski • *Hidden Figures* by Margot Lee Shetterly & Laura Freeman	• Peter Thorpe	• 3D model-making • Pastel drawing
Year 5/6			
Cycle 1 Autumn Term	• *The Arrival* by Shaun Tan	• Shaun Tan • Albrecht Durer	• Drawing
Cycle 1 Spring Term	• *Letters from the Lighthouse* by Emma Carroll • *Hello, Lighthouse* by Sophie Blackall	• Sophie Blackall • Katsushika Hokusai • Winslow Homer	• Mixed-media
Cycle 2 Autumn Term	• *The Lost Words* by Robert MacFarlane & Jackie Morris	• Jackie Morris	• Drawing and painting
Cycle 2 Spring Term	• *The Storm Keeper's Island* by Catherine Doyle	• Sarkasi Said	• Textile design

Term	Inspirational books	Extraordinary lives: artists	Art focus
Cycle 2 Summer Term	• *Who Let the Gods Out* by Maz Evans • *Greek Gods & Heroes* by Sylvie Baussier & Almasty • *Wilma Unlimited* by Kathleen Krull • *Mythologica* by Steve Kershaw & Victoria Topping		• Sculpture • Collage

Curriculum case study 2: designing a primary art curriculum that uses critical analysis, sequenced knowledge about art and the skills to make art

Rachel A. MacInnes, art and design lead at St Paul's Catholic Primary School, Northumberland

A reflection on the process and impact of redesigning our art and design curriculum

To promote the value of the subject, provide access to cultural heritage for our pupils, improve the skills and confidence of staff and create a school culture of independent pupil artists

Planning

I took over the role of Art and Design Subject Lead in the Spring Term of 2020. Our school had been through a significant period of change in both structure and staffing; our curriculum had borne the resulting stresses and strains. It wasn't what we wanted for our provision. Art and design; craft; and design and technology were all blurred together and the content of the curriculum (both knowledge and skills) was disconnected – both from the rest of our curriculum and from the progressive steps that build a successful artist. Staff knowledge was inconsistent, and art and design was predominantly seen as painting a nice picture at the end of a topic. I decided to start completely anew.

I began from what I loved – inspirational pieces of art. I wanted to give all pupils in our school access to and ownership of their cultural heritage of art. I wanted them to know that it belonged to them, could speak to them, could help them to understand the world and themselves. I separated art and design; design and technology; and craft into three distinct, but complimentary, areas of learning, with separate slots on the timetable and assigned workbooks for each subject. I worked with staff to clarify their understanding of art as a subject worthy of teaching in its own right; of craft-driven enrichment opportunities and experiences; and of the valuable opportunities for these to intersect but not dilute.

New leadership at our school encouraged staff to take ownership of the whole curriculum: to be designed for our pupils, in our school. A whole new focus was agreed and implemented, using individual figures for each year group and each term as a lens to filter the rest of the curriculum. I began by selecting artworks that would enrich each lens: 'Starry Night' by Van Gogh with the astronaut Tim Peake in Year 5, 'Queen Elizabeth II' by Andy Warhol with Queen Elizabeth in Year 2, 'Peter Rabbit' by Beatrix Potter with Traditional Tales. This led to a set of foundational artworks that would mean each pupil leaving our school would have a working knowledge and critical understanding of these core pieces.

Some figures were more challenging than others to match and, where I had to make a choice between matching the lens and sacrificing the quality of art, I always prioritised the quality of the art. Mostly this meant I simply broadened the lens to encompass the theme or value exemplified by the focus figure; it also meant that the choices stood on their own feet. Should a shift of curriculum design focus be initiated in the future, these artworks would be able to fight for their place on their own merits.

There are limits to how much content can be covered in a set period of time, but I wanted to ensure that the artistic voices being present were as diverse and wide ranging as possible. We are a one-form entry primary school in rural Northumberland, so it is essential in our role as subject leaders that we build diversity of artists alongside art form into the curriculum. To support this aim, I decided to support each core artwork with two supplementary pieces. This helped to achieve a balance between historically established artists (Picasso, Van Gogh, Monet) and less universally well-known creators (Cath Read, David Best, Rosa Bonheur).

Now I was ready to plan out the art skills, processes and outcomes that I wanted for our pupils as they worked through the curriculum. Using the national curriculum framework and leaning on the research and experience of the NSEAD resources, Paul Carney and the knowledgeable community of art teachers on X (formerly Twitter), I selected the final outcomes for each unit and the skills building to that outcome. Ensuring a balance of painting, drawing, printing, sculpture and digital art was woven through the units, allowing for revision of previously taught concepts and skills, meant that identified gaps could be filled and opportunities for pupils to select independently and confidently from an increasing set of creative tools were optimised.

Key to this aim would be introducing the use of sketchbooks for art and design. Sketchbooks are an essential part of my own artist teacher practice, and I knew they would be transformative to the way we taught art and the perceived value of that subject. I also knew they would be the biggest challenge for staff who were unsure of their own artistic skills – their previous reliance on online video tutorials to teach pupils core skills was evidence of this. To ameliorate this, I created a sketchbook for each unit I taught, to share with staff and pupils, working as both a model and a trial before the curriculum was put into practice.

I was aware that presenting an entirely new, whole-school curriculum for art and design would create both opportunities and challenges for staff. I wanted to keep workload to a minimum, build enthusiasm around the subject and keep staff energy for teaching pupils art rather than getting bogged down in planning and progression. To support this, alongside the usual long-term and medium-term plans, I created outcome overviews for each unit. These placed the core artwork at the heart of the unit and provided an easy-to-use guide to the steps leading to the final piece. I also included vocabulary (subject and tier two) using resources from Emma Stanley's work on vocabulary and the Jane Considine approach to book talk. I needed to shift the current school culture from regarding art as a purely 'making' subject to an observational, critical-thinking opportunity; embedding it in our work on improving the quality of partner talk seemed an effective way to do this. Picture Talk resources for each unit supported and modelled this for staff.

Implementation

By September 2021, everything was in place to roll out to staff and pupils: planning, progression, resources, training and coaching. After working on it all for so long, I was really excited to see how it would work in our school. The primary curriculum is an unwieldy creature, and teachers are often pulled between equally important but conflicting pressures. I wanted to present the art and design curriculum as a minimal effort, maximum value opportunity for staff and pupils.

The new curriculum was well received by staff, and they threw themselves into getting it started. I actively checked in with all staff, both in person and online, to see how they were finding it, offer suggestions to adapt or mitigate challenges and offer support where needed. Pupils responded so positively to it – talking about art, using the sketchbooks, composing personal responses – that the curriculum really did the work for me now.

I was teaching the curriculum myself, so I got to see its effects firsthand. To make best use of my own skills, the senior leadership team introduced an opportunity for me to teach art and design across KS2, so I was teaching at least one unit in each year group from Year 3 to Year 6 across an academic year. It also meant that KS2 teachers could see the impact of the curriculum and teaching approach within their own class.

The Year 6 unit was a challenge to plan and creatively satisfying to teach. As a subject that can tend to the conventional in primary, I wanted to attempt to provoke a more complex response from pupils. I selected 'Hurricane in Flight' by Eric Ravillious as its core artwork and covered perspective, line drawing, collage and digital art within the skill content. The class covers World War II in history, and their English work is also based on texts around this theme, meaning pupils have a developing contextual knowledge that can be enriched and built upon within the art sessions.

Each lesson across the curriculum involves sketchbook tasks, art analysis and creative composition. There are six sessions to each unit, following a sequenced structure: observe, experience, imagine, create, refine and reflect. This allows for a fluid model, support and challenge approach. Teachers directly teach a skill, then support pupils to use it independently, making choices about how best to use these skills in their final pieces. Evaluation and analysis are built in as part of the creative process.

The introduction of sketchbooks brought the curriculum to life. It created a complete cultural shift in the way staff and pupils viewed their own artist practice – allowing for experimentation, reviewing, revising, recreating and the ability to witness their own progress. This was especially evident in the World War II unit in Year 6, where pupils really began to take ownership of their sketchbook, making purposeful choices as part of an evolving, evaluative process. The resulting final pieces have an individual identity that reflects this process, placing the emphasis on response and creation rather than replication.

The curriculum is in its third year now and no units have been changed, although I am starting to adjust the activities to allow for the improving skill level of pupils. The pupils I teach for art and design in Year 6 now are very different from the Year 6 class I first taught this curriculum to. Their use of sketchbooks is confident and personal; they almost instinctively seem to experiment with colour, medium and composition. They understand outcomes in art are not fixed but move with their own intention and developing response to a subject or stimulus. They talk articulately about the contexts of a piece of art, the choices of the artist and their own response to that art. The culture among the staff has shifted from seeing art and design as a means of production to a way of allowing pupils to experience and understand the world, as fundamental to their development as reading and writing.

Curriculum case study 3: a curriculum centred around the principles of LOVE (Long-term memory, Oracy-rich, Values-based and Experiential learning)

Charlotte Ford, Specialist Teacher for The Flying High Trust

Cotgrave Candleby Lane School is a large primary within Nottinghamshire and a member of The Flying High Partnership. In our most recent Ofsted inspection (December 2023), we were graded 'Outstanding' and were proud to showcase our art curriculum as one of the deep-dive subjects.

One of our school values is creativity, and therefore art and design is an integral part of our curriculum. We have worked closely with Flying High to develop an enquiry-based curriculum that gives art and design a high status. This has been enhanced by our time working as the Nottinghamshire Education Partner for The Mighty Creatives, where we gained further expertise when supporting other schools with their curriculum and Artsmark journeys.

Our pupils are always at the heart of everything we do, and therefore it was important to construct our curriculum carefully to enable them to have high aspirations and see themselves as artists.

We want to ensure our pupils are supported to have a genuine love of learning. Our curriculum is broad and balanced, rich and varied, and provides them with experiences and opportunities that are relevant and meaningful. Not only are we committed to ensuring our pupils are ready for the next stage in their education, but that they are also prepared to take their place in a truly global society.

Our curriculum is centred around the principles of LOVE, which stands for: Long-term memory, Oracy-rich, Values-based and Experiential learning. Our LOVE principles ensure that our pupils learn and remember a wide schema of knowledge; develop strong language and communication skills; embody values to live by; and have regular firsthand learning opportunities to ensure their learning is memorable.

'I can't draw!'

Before implementation, we were determined to create a mindset shift to help all pupils to see that there is no right or wrong in the art world. This culture had to be role-modelled by our teaching staff to provide consistent messages.

Learning about artists is integral to our curriculum; however, we firmly believe that it is important to go beyond simply replicating the work of famous artists. Indeed, this forms part of the learning process, but should not be seen as an end point. It is vital pupils are nurtured to experiment, take risks and make their own decisions about their use of media and technique to achieve a desired outcome. This critical-thinking is essential for pupils to develop their originality. Furthermore, we believe pupils should be taught about a range of artists, craft-makers, designers and architects of all different walks of life, backgrounds and diversities. Pupils should feel encouraged that art is for everybody and that there should be no barriers to this.

Design and implementation of our curriculum

Our school curriculum is delivered through an enquiry approach, where pupils have an overarching question to structure their learning each term. We deliver at the least the expectations of the EYFS curriculum and the national curriculum, and in some cases exceed these expectations, such as the use of sketchbooks across all year groups. We have used nationally recognised resources such as Access Art and NSEAD to support our thinking.

The composite knowledge we teach across school, from F1 to Y6, is organised into Key Knowledge Progression Documents (KKPDs) for each national curriculum subject. Substantive, procedural and disciplinary knowledge is organised into strands for each subject in each KKPD. These KKPDs are organised into a long-term plan and subject maps to ensure that our learning is progressive and linked across year groups and subjects through deliberate content choices. Knowledge identified on the KKPDs is linked to Component Knowledge Progression Documents (CKPDs) for each subject.

Termly, the KKPDs are used to plan out sequences of granular learning using our medium-term planning documents. Knowledge statements are skilfully transferred into sequences of learning objectives that build, day by day and week by week, to answer the enquiry question. This authentic outcome to the enquiry allows pupils to answer the question in a way that enables them to demonstrate their learning and knowledge gained from the enquiry; produce high-quality work that answers the question; share their answer to the question with an audience wider than the school; and also leave a social legacy beyond their classroom and their school.

We teach three enquiries in an academic year, each enquiry lasting for one term. Each enquiry has an overarching enquiry question, and the granular learning sequence for each enquiry develops pupils' knowledge and skills to be able to answer the enquiry question at the end of the term through the enquiry authentic outcome. We recognise that our pupils must learn knowledge first to be able to develop new skills.

Each enquiry has a driver subject:

- Autumn term – history
- Spring term – geography
- Summer term – art and design

For each enquiry, there are identified enhancer subjects with knowledge and skills for pupils to learn that enhances their driver subject knowledge and helps them to answer the enquiry question through their authentic outcome. Art acts as a valuable enhancer subject, particularly during the autumn term to support the history enquiry.

Moreover, our carefully designed curriculum is assessed through the enquiries. Pupils can recall substantive knowledge and draw upon procedural learning during the weekly 'Leitner' or 'Plickers' quizzes. This helps our pupils to commit key teaching points into their long-term memory and recall them in future lessons.

Design and implementation of our art and design curriculum

When mapping out our content choices on the Art and Design Subject Map, we decided that, each term, pupils will study a particular strand of the curriculum, such as painting, drawing or sculpture. We wanted to ensure that 'Knowledge of artists' was a thread throughout every term, as well as running the 'Elements of art' alongside. To make our artist content choices, we researched artists from different time periods, localities and diversities. We also used AccessArt and NSEAD to support our decision-making. When mapping these choices across the school, we thought carefully about where links could be made, and how teachers could reactivate prior knowledge taught in previous year groups.

Key concepts and techniques are revisited multiple times to allow pupils to build on their current understanding, enabling them to develop interconnected webs of knowledge as a schema. Consequently, they can make purposeful connections to think more deeply. Our subject map details the current, prior and subsequent knowledge for each term in every year group. This supports our staff to understand the content choices, where links can be made and, therefore, knowledge transferred. For example, in KS1, our pupils learn about the abstract sculptures of Barbara Hepworth. They recall this understanding in KS2 to discuss how her work influenced the sculptor Henry Moore.

To build staff confidence in creating art learning sequences, we developed our own 'Art and Design Learning Sequence Model'. We often compare an art sequence to the likeness of a writing sequence. For example, you would often begin an English sequence by learning about a particular author, book or 'WAGOLL' text. Then you might unpick the features used, develop grammatical skills and move onto planning, drafting and editing, before creating a published piece of writing. In the same way that writing is a journey and can always be edited, we wanted our staff to see that art follows a similar structure. By making this link clear, it helped to unlock their understanding, as many felt uncertain how to map out the necessary lessons order effectively.

Our art sequence follows this structure:

1 **Immersion in the artist or art movement**

   Introduce and share the artist or art movement. Pupils learn about the chosen artist, their personal background and influences. They learn about the artist's place in history, culture or links to diversity. They begin to explore the work of the chosen artist, craft-maker, designer or architect. They identify links to artists they have learned about previously, commenting on similarities and differences. They comment on what they like or dislike and give reasons for this. At this stage, substantive knowledge about the artist is shared.

2 **Identifying artistic features**

   Pupils look at examples of the artist's work – what is the artist's intent? They comment on the art elements used (colour, pattern, texture, line, shape, space) and the composition of the pieces. They compare and contrast different works. They must be able to articulate the common themes, media and techniques used and why, to answer the question: What is the meaning behind these choices?

3 **Recreate**

Pupils have a go at recreating and interpreting a famous artwork by their chosen artist. They learn how to recreate a famous piece, modelled in step-by-step stages. This encourages them to make purposeful observations about the style and techniques used. It is essential that the sequence does not end with replicating another artist's work as pupils must be given the opportunity to innovate and apply taught techniques afterwards.

4 **Techniques and processes**

Pupils develop technical knowledge that makes their own artwork successful. They learn new or specific techniques to apply later in the sequence. This is an opportunity to focus on developing procedural knowledge. They use their sketchbooks as a space to explore and experiment with these techniques, as well as with different media. They record their thought processes, commenting on what has been successful or unsuccessful and why.

5 **Innovation: design and plan**

Pupils are inspired by their artist and design their own piece of art in this style. They will develop their independence at this stage by making deliberate choices about which art elements, techniques and media to use. They experiment throughout this process, not limited to creating only one design. They record this process in their sketchbooks and critique their ideas until a final design has been chosen. This is an opportunity to apply procedural knowledge and develop disciplinary knowledge.

6 **Create**

Pupils apply both their procedural and disciplinary knowledge to create their final piece. Influences from the artist studied are evident in their outcome. They adapt their choices as needed, applying a range of techniques and considering the art elements. This piece is likely to be created outside of the sketchbook and on a larger scale, showing more accuracy and precision.

7 **Analyse and evaluate**

Pupils analyse and evaluate their final piece: Has the artwork met the artist's intended purpose? They use different methods to critique their artwork, including the use of peer feedback. They reflect on their stylistic choices, commenting on what has worked well and what they may have done differently. They articulate how their artwork has been influenced by the artist, historical period, diversity links or culture studied. They consider how their artwork will be displayed to a wider audience to be celebrated, such as part of a school exhibition.

This sequence has hugely improved our staff confidence in writing granular art sequences. It provides a tight structure that allows time for pupils to explore their creativity purposefully, as well as to develop their substantive, procedural and disciplinary knowledge. Now it is an embedded part of our curriculum, our pupils are familiar with the sequence and are therefore becoming more independent with the creative learning process.

Sketchbooks

We believe that the use of sketchbooks is fundamental to learning about art and design as they provide pupils with a safe space to be creative, experiment and risk-take. This is not limited to drawing or testing out painting techniques, but is also a space to make notes and provide written evaluations about their learning journeys. Sketchbooks should feel like a safe space for pupils and not a space for judgement. We like to use the term 'arts log' as this encourages pupils to see their books as an ongoing record of their creative-thinking. Determined to go beyond the expectations set out by the national curriculum, our pupils' sketchbook journeys begin when they are in Reception.

To achieve consistency and progression across school, we produced an expectations document for our approach to sketchbooks as well as exemplification to support staff, including Early Career Teachers. This ensures that pupils' creative work and thinking continues to be aspirational as they move through school and prepare for secondary school.

Impact on pupils and the subject as a whole

Since implementing our art curriculum, there has been a significant shift in the growth mindset of our pupils. Not only do they have a great knowledge of artists and techniques, but they are confident at trying out new ideas and ways of thinking, which leads them to produce their own interpretations and original pieces of artwork. Furthermore, we have noticed that, within the analysing and evaluating aspect of the learning sequence, pupils are far more resilient at giving and accepting critical feedback. They are eager to ensure their artwork continues to be the best it can be.

Our sketchbooks have evolved over time as our pupils are becoming more and more confident in how to use them effectively. Something we are most proud of is how pupils now choose to set out their work within sketchbooks. At the start of our journey, they were very reliant on modelling by the teacher and would present their learning identically. Now pupils are incredibly independent and make individual choices about what and how to present their creative-thinking. For example, pupils learning about Banksy decided to cut up the bottom of their sketchbook page to represent the shredding stunt that took place or chose only monochrome tones with pops of red, therefore showing a secure understanding of the artist's style. Question marks would even fill their pages to represent his anonymity. This independent thinking has been achieved by staff having their own sketchbooks, modelling under a visualiser and verbalising their choices as they make them. As a result, pupils see critical-thinking and feel comfortable to do the same.

Not only did we want to increase pupil confidence with the use of sketchbooks, but we allocated staff meeting slots to support teachers with how to use them effectively in the classroom. As a result, we developed a shared clarity and helped staff to feel empowered. It is now common practice that all teachers keep their own sketchbooks, from which they model their decision-making under a visualiser during lessons.

During our Ofsted inspection in December 2023, we were delighted to be graded 'Outstanding', with the report stating that 'the curriculum flows seamlessly', is 'extremely well designed' and that 'the order in which pupils learn new knowledge and information is crystal clear', resulting in pupils having a 'rich and deep body of knowledge over time'.

During the inspection, art was chosen as a deep-dive subject. For each deep dive, the inspectors held discussions about the curriculum, visited a sample of lessons, spoke to teachers, spoke to some pupils about their learning and looked at samples of pupils' work. Pupils talked with confidence to the inspectors about their knowledge of substantive, procedural and disciplinary knowledge in art and design. They recalled knowledge from previous years and could articulate the links to the current learning. Furthermore, they took great pride in talking through their sketchbooks, making it clear they had full ownership of them.

The visits to lessons were an integral part of showcasing the impact our art curriculum has had. Pupils in EYFS showed their 'thirst for learning' as they articulated their artist knowledge. The inspector acknowledged how well pupils were accessing art learning within their outdoor provision and overheard a conversation between two reception pupils discussing the artist Georgia O'Keeffe. During the interviews with pupils in KS2, they talked with confidence about their learning sequences within sketchbooks, drawing upon techniques and artist knowledge. Additionally, they could articulate how their learning in previous years builds onto their learning in the next.

Our growing examples of pupils' work are now being implemented into our own exemplification of the curriculum KKPDs. This will help staff to maintain expectations and progression across the different strands.

Summary

The commonality between these three case studies, despite their contrasting starting points, is a shared belief that the national curriculum descriptors should be seen as a foundation rather than a limitation. Karl Duke uses reading as the inspiration for Blyton cum Laughton's curriculum; Rachel MacInnes uses a lens-based approach to design the curriculum at St Paul's; and Charlotte Ford uses LOVE principles as the framework for curriculum-planning at Cotgrave Candleby Lane. Each builds outwards from the same brief set of statements set out in the national curriculum (and reproduced at the start of this chapter), but each looks completely different. That is absolutely how it should be.

In the chapters that follow, we move from thinking about the architecture of your curriculum to the nuts and bolts of planning and teaching it.

Further reading

AccessArt: Inspiring the Teaching and Learning of Visual Arts [online] Available at: www.accessart.org.uk (Accessed: 16 May 2026).

Counsell, C. (2018) 'Taking curriculum seriously' on Impact, 4 [online] Available at: https://my.chartered.college/impact_article/taking-curriculum-seriously (Accessed: 16 May 2026).

DfE (2013) *Art and design programmes of study: key stages 1 and 2* [online] Available at: https://assets.publishing.service.gov.uk/media/5a7ba810ed915d4147621ca0/PRIMARY_national_curriculum_-_Art_and_design.pdf (Accessed: 12 July 2026).

Gomersal Primary School Art Blog [online] Available at: https://gomersalprimaryschoolart.blogspot.com (Accessed: 14 May 2026).

NSEAD 'Our manifesto for art, craft and design education' [online] Available at: https://www.nsead.org/community-activism/advocacy/nseads-2024-manifesto/ (Accessed 27 July 2026).

CHAPTER 5
SAMPLE PLANNING SEQUENCE

The different stages of planning

There are several thought processes and stages that need to be worked through before detailed planning begins and sequences of learning delivered to pupils. The national curriculum comes first, which feeds into whole-school art and design curriculum and progression-map development. From these, sequences of learning can be devised and individual lessons curated.

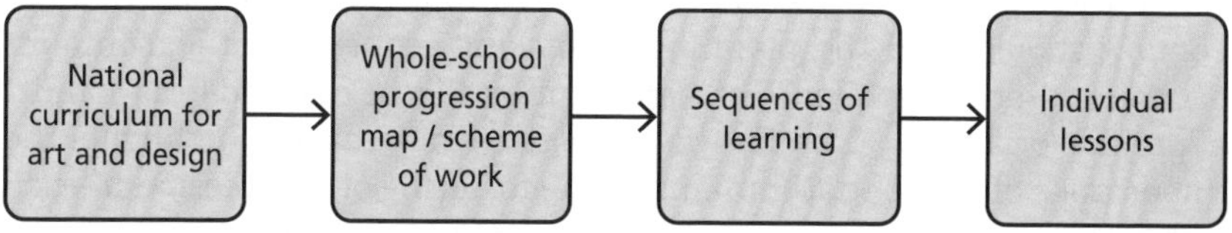

▲ **Figure 5.1 The different stages of planning**

Planning a sequence of learning can seem overwhelming. But breaking it down into small steps and asking a few key questions when embarking on the process can help develop and clarify thinking. I'm a bit old-fashioned at this stage and like nothing more than a large sheet of paper, pens and sticky notes to scribble on. I jot down any ideas that pop into my head. Not everything I contemplate at this stage ends up in the final sequence. Of course, this is by no means the only way of carrying out initial planning; many teachers choose to work digitally or with a more structured template, but this is the way that worked for me during my time in the classroom.

The following useful questions are important to consider at this early planning phase:

- Which year group am I planning for and what previous art experiences have the pupils had?
- What area of making does this sequence develop?
- What key knowledge and skills do I want pupils to acquire?
- What stimuli will pupils be given?

- Are there any relevant artists to share during this sequence? How do they fit into the learning?
- Which tools and media will be needed? Do I have them in school?
- What might the processes and products look like during this sequence?
- What relevant and engaging experiences will pupils partake in?
- What outcomes am I hoping pupils will produce?
- What is the timeframe for the project and how many sessions / hours will it be taught over?
- Do I have pupils who will need the learning adapted?
- How am I going to assess the learning?
- How are pupils going to be given the opportunity to reflect during the sequence?

As mentioned previously, a school's overarching art and design curriculum content should feed the planning of specific sequences of learning for each year group. A sequence of learning may also be referred to as a 'unit', a 'project' or a 'topic'. I prefer the *sequence* term because it highlights the importance of sequential thinking in the fostering of progression in each pupil. The sequences I usually plan consist of five or six lessons (or stages of learning) lasting around an hour each, but there is no hard or fast rule that states this is the way it must be done. Indeed, I've worked with schools that successfully teach three larger sequences of ten lessons per academic year and schools that effectively block art and design and teach it for three whole afternoons every half term. As we've discussed before in this book, there is no one-size-fits-all ruling for the subject and it's important that we create a culture and routine suitable for each school context. There are many routes to the intended outcomes of the primary art and design curriculum; ultimately, these outcomes are the artistic progression of all pupils and the development of confident young artists.

We discuss in Chapter 3 the three domains of art and design knowledge – practical, theoretical and disciplinary – and sequences of learning should have elements to them that develop each of these areas woven throughout, although some units may be more heavily weighted in the direction of one or more of them. Artists and artworks can be used to inspire pupils; practical skills can be taught and the opportunity to explore and experiment should be provided. Alongside this knowledge acquisition, pupils also need to be allowed the time to think and work creatively and to reflect and evaluate as they journey through a unit.

When beginning to plan out a sequence, teachers need to refer to the national curriculum, and their school's art and design curriculum and progression map. It's important to remember that progression maps are successful only if there is buy-in from a whole-school team; if that's not there, gaps in learning will occur and lead to a breakdown in progression. It's important to be aware of the content delivered to a cohort in previous years and the intended coverage for future years. This ensures that the planned, small stepping stones of progression support each pupil: take one away, and they fall in the river or jump too far to reach the next stone, leaving gaps in learning. Likewise, staying on one step for too long leaves pupils stuck in that one spot, repeating content over and over again. It is imperative that every teacher in every year group uses the progression map (as well as the previous teacher's notes and assessment of a cohort) to inform their planning.

Initial overview

The outline of the intended learning for a sequence – what teachers want pupils to know, be able to do and remember – needs to be identified first. The following intended outcomes are taken from the Haringey Education Partnership art and design curriculum; specifically, the Year 1 'Exploring colour' sequence. In this sequence, pupils explore the world of colour. They are introduced to the primary and secondary colour wheels and experiment with colour mixing. They learn that colours can be described as 'warm' or 'cool' and look at examples of artwork using colour for this purpose.

Intended sequence outcomes

Pupils will be able to:

- talk about and describe their favourite colours
- name the primary and secondary colours
- explore colour-mixing with confidence
- mix primary-colour paints to make secondary-colour paints
- recognise and be able to talk about the primary and secondary colour wheels
- spot primary and secondary colours in their environment
- use a variety of brushes and tools to apply paint accurately to their sketchbook pages

- create collections of colours
- understand that colours can be described as 'warm' / 'cool' or 'hot' / 'cold'
- recognise primary colours in a relevant artist's work
- apply their colour-mixing knowledge and skills to their own piece of artwork.

Key vocabulary

It is important to think about the key subject-specific vocabulary pupils are going to be introduced to and use in context during the sequence. Being aware of this before embarking on individual lesson plans will ensure that they are included in the teaching and learning. The key vocabulary identified for this 'Exploring colour' sequence follows:

colour colour wheel primary colour secondary colour red yellow blue green orange purple indigo violet paint painting print printing brush mix mixing warm colour hot colour cool colour cold colour pattern shape rainbow

Skills and knowledge

By the end of this sequence, pupils will know that…

- colour is one of the key elements of art
- red, yellow and blue are primary colours
- there are primary and secondary colour wheels
- primary colours mix to make secondary colours
- red and yellow make orange
- yellow and blue make green
- blue and red make purple
- orange, green and purple are secondary colours
- indigo is a blue purple
- violet is a red purple
- colours can be described as warm or cool
- red, yellow and orange are warm colours
- blue, green and purple are cool colours.

Key skills

By the end of this sequence, pupils will have the skills to:

- print with everyday objects
- use a ruler to draw straight lines
- talk about a piece of artwork in terms of the colours used
- explore mixing colours
- mix colours for a purpose
- use a paintbrush to mix colours with control and accuracy
- use a paintbrush to paint a curved line with control.

The lesson sequence

After creating an overview, teachers can then plot out a rough guide to each lesson before embarking on the planning of each one in detail, for example:

1 **What is a primary colour?**

In this session, pupils will learn that red, yellow and blue are the primary colours. They will explore painting and printing in their sketchbooks using them and hunt for them in their immediate environment.

2 **Primary colours in works of art**

In this session, pupils will be introduced to the paintings of Dutch artist Piet Mondrian and will spot the primary colours in his artwork. Pupils will then create their own primary-colour paintings inspired by his compositions using pencils, rulers, paintbrushes and red, yellow, blue and black paint.

3 **Colour-mixing discoveries**

In this session, pupils will explore what happens if you mix two primary colours together. They will mix red with yellow; red with blue; and yellow with blue, using their fingers and hands. They will learn the term 'secondary colour' and be introduced to the primary and secondary colour wheels.

4 **Painting rainbows**

In this session, pupils will apply their knowledge of primary and secondary colours to paint their own rainbow compositions from the primary colours. They will also learn how to mix indigo and violet using different ratios of red and blue paint.

5 **Warm and cool colours**

In this session, pupils will learn that half the colours on the secondary colour wheel can be described as 'warm' (red, yellow, orange) and the other half described as 'cool' (blue, green, purple). They will discuss why this is and how the colours make them feel, before making their own warm and cool colour collections.

6 **Colour-collection flat-lay photography**

In this session, pupils will create colour collections of their choice and arrange them for flat-lay photographs to be taken using a camera or tablet.

Cross-referencing the sequence outline with the national curriculum descriptors for the key stage is a useful exercise to ensure pupils are being taught the intended core content.

Once the skeleton outline for the whole unit is formed, it's time to take each lesson in turn and decide on the most appropriate way to deliver the planned experiences and knowledge to pupils.

Lesson 1

This first lesson is an introduction to the primary colours; it is also designed as an early autumn-term art lesson for pupils moving up from EYFS to Year 1. It is the first time these pupils will have been introduced to a sketchbook, so part of the lesson focuses on this.

Table 5.1 Exploring colour: Lesson 1

Objectives
• To talk about and describe favourite colours • To know that red, yellow and blue are the primary colours • To use brushes and tools to apply paint to paper carefully and accurately • To spot primary colours in the environment
Key vocabulary
colour red yellow blue primary colour paint print paintbrush sketchbook
Equipment required
• Lesson PowerPoint slides • Printout for sketchbooks • Glue • Sketchbooks • Ready-mixed paint • Paintbrushes (various sizes) • Objects for printing • Paint palettes
Retrieval and context-setting
Begin this lesson by singing 'I can sing a rainbow' with your class. Explain that today's lesson is all about colour. Colour makes the world a beautiful place. Open up a discussion about colour using questions displayed on the whiteboard or asked orally one at a time; pupils can talk in pairs, groups or as a whole class. • Do you have a favourite colour? • How does your favourite colour make you feel? • Can you spot your favourite colour in the classroom?
New learning
Show pupils the colours red, yellow and blue on the whiteboard. Ask them to name the colours as they appear on the screen. Introduce them to the term *primary colour*. There are three primary colours. Red is a primary colour, yellow is a primary colour and blue is a primary colour. From these three primary colours, it is possible to make a huge range of different colours. Introduce the primary-colour wheel.

Pupil discovery and application

Introduce the idea of sketchbooks. Sketchbooks are books that artists use to explore, try out their ideas and make discoveries in. Pupils will be using sketchbooks in their art lessons and working like artists because *that is what they are!*

Prepare the classroom for painting and printing exploration. Provide pupils with sketchbooks; ready-mixed paint in red, blue and yellow; various sized paintbrushes; and objects for printing with, such as sponges, building blocks, lids, corks and cotton reels. Cover the tables and ask pupils to put aprons on.

Demonstrate the activity process step by step, either via a prerecorded video or live. Pupils are to fill their allocated sketchbook pages with primary-colour paint in any way they choose to. Encourage pupils to discuss their choices and techniques while they are creating their pages. Invite pupils to talk about their favourite primary colours. Can they justify and articulate their choices?

- 'My favourite primary colour is red because it reminds me of strawberries: I really like strawberries.'
- 'My favourite primary colour is blue because it reminds me of the ocean: I love the sound of the waves.'
- 'Yellow is my favourite primary colour because it is bright and cheerful like the sun.'

Reflection time

Finish today's session with a recap of the primary colours and a linked game of I-spy:

- 'I spy with my little eye something red.'
- 'I spy with my little eye something blue.'
- 'I spy with my little eye something yellow.'

Assessment opportunities

- **Through observation:** Can pupils hold the tools and paintbrushes comfortably to make marks? Can pupils apply paint with control to their sketchbook pages?
- **Through discussion:** Can pupils name the three primary colours? Can pupils identify red, yellow and blue items in the classroom?

Lesson 2

This second lesson gives pupils the opportunity to see how an artist has used the primary colours in their artwork. Dutch artist Piet Mondrian is used to inspire pupils, but there are other historical and contemporary artists who also used the primary colours, who could be referenced instead.

▼ **Table 5.2 Exploring colour: Lesson 2**

Objectives • To recognise the primary colours in a piece of artwork • To describe the work of the Dutch artist Piet Mondrian • To use a ruler to draw straight lines • To work carefully and accurately when painting
Key vocabulary colour red yellow blue primary colour black artist Piet Mondrian Dutch square rectangle line straight shape abstract geometric
Equipment required • Lesson PowerPoint slides • Sketchbooks or cartridge paper • Ready-mixed paint in red, yellow, blue and black • Paintbrushes (various sizes) • Rulers • Paint palettes
Retrieval and context-setting Ask pupils whether they can remember the primary colours. Play a 'sorting colours' game. Show a variety of objects of different colours on the whiteboard or put a selection on the desks for pupils to sort physically. Which of the objects are primary colours and which are not? Sort them into two groups. Explain that, today, pupils are going to be learning about a famous artist who liked to paint with the primary colours. Check pupils understanding of the term *artist*. An artist is a person who creates art.

New learning

As a class, explore the artwork of Dutch artist Piet Mondrian. He was an abstract artist who lived from 1872 to 1944. Abstract art is a form of art that has no recognisable subject, such as a living thing or object. Instead, abstract artists like Mondrian communicate their ideas, thoughts and feelings through colours, lines and shapes. Look at some of Mondrian's artworks, such as these:

- 'Composition with Red, Yellow and Blue' (1935 / 1942)
- 'Composition No.12 with Blue' (1936 / 1942)
- 'Broadway Boogie Woogie' (1942–43)

While looking at the artwork, ask pupils the following questions:

- What colours can you see?
- Can you spot the primary colours?
- What words could you use to describe the lines in Mondrian's work?
- What words would you use to describe the shapes in Mondrian's artwork?
- What is the same about these three pieces of artwork? What is different?
- Do you like his paintings? Why?

Pupil discovery and application

In this lesson, pupils are going to create their own primary-colour artwork using squares, rectangles and straight lines in the style of Piet Mondrian. Prepare the classroom for painting. Give the pupils their sketchbooks or cartridge paper; pencils; rulers; paint palettes with red, blue, yellow and black ready-mixed paint; and paintbrushes. It is a good idea to allocate brushes to each colour paint to avoid unwanted colour-mixing and the need to wash brushes during the activity.

Ask pupils to follow these step-by-step painting instructions:

1. Draw a geometric pattern of straight lines, squares and rectangles on the paper or page of a sketchbook using a ruler and a pencil.
2. Paint the shapes created using paint in the primary colours. (If pupils choose to, they can leave some shapes white.)
3. Leave to part dry, then paint over the lines using a thin paintbrush and black paint.

Reflection time

Ask pupils to leave their paintings on the table and to walk around the classroom looking at and admiring the artwork that has been created during the lesson. Encourage them to talk about what they like in the artwork created by their peers.

Assessment opportunities
• **Through observation:** Can pupils hold their paintbrush to paint with control and accuracy? Can pupils use a ruler to draw straight lines? • **Through discussion:** Can pupils talk about the shapes and colours they can see in the artwork? Can pupils use the term *primary colour* in context?

Lesson 3

In this next lesson, pupils explore mixing primary colours to create secondary colours. This lesson plan sees pupils colour-mixing with their hands. If this doesn't suit your class or setting, there are lots of other ways to colour-mix too: mixing powder paint in puddles, mixing ready-mixed paint in palettes, mixing paint in squishy bags, and more.

▼ **Table 5.3 Exploring colour: Lesson 3**

Objectives
• To experiment with mixing paint • To use a brush with control to mix paint and coat hands • To know that two primary colours can be mixed to create a secondary colour • To know that green, orange and purple are the secondary colours
Key vocabulary
red yellow blue primary colour orange green purple secondary colour mix print colour wheel
Equipment required
• Lesson PowerPoint slides • Sketchbooks • Ready-mixed paint in red, yellow and blue • Paintbrushes • Paint palettes
Retrieval and context-setting
Show pupils the 'Composition with Red, Yellow and Blue' (1935 / 1942) by Piet Mondrian. Encourage pupils to discuss the concepts covered in the last session: line, shape and colour. Explain that, in this week's session, they will be using the primary colours again, but this time to mix new colours.

New learning

Show pupils the primary colours on the teaching slides (or hold up bottles of paint or pieces of paper in each colour) and explain that, from these three colours, other colours can be made: by taking equal amounts of two of the primary colours, a secondary colour can be created.

Pupil discovery and application

In this lesson, pupils explore mixing primary colours to create secondary colours. Set up the classroom for messy painting. Cover the tables with cloths or newspaper and ask pupils to put aprons on. Each table will need ready-mixed paint in red, blue and yellow, paint palettes and paintbrushes. Each pupil will need their sketchbook open on its next double page.

Pupils should choose a colour to paint the palm of one hand with, then choose a different second colour to paint the palm of the other hand with (pupils can work in pairs to do this). They can then print each colour hand on a page in their sketchbook.

They should rub their hands together to mix the remaining paint in their palms – this will create their secondary colour. They should then print this secondary colour in their sketchbooks next to the two primary colours that mixed to create it. Repeat this activity using different colour combinations. Encourage pupils to talk about the process and their discoveries as they work.

Pupils can also explore colour-mixing using their fingertips. Dip two fingers in different primary colour paints and mix them together to create a secondary colour.

If pupils are uncomfortable with the feel of the paint on their skin, provide palettes for them to mix the colours in using a brush.

After making their own discoveries, show slides of the different primary-colour combinations and discuss the secondary colour they combine to make. Introduce the secondary-colour wheel. Show the primary-colour wheel first, then the secondary-colour wheel. What do pupils spot between each primary colour on the secondary colour wheel? (The secondary colour they combine to make.)

Pupils should discover that:

- red and yellow make orange
- yellow and blue make green
- red and blue make purple.

Ask pupils to spot objects in the classroom the same hue as the secondary colour being discussed.

Reflection time
Ask pupils what they have discovered during the session. Share colour calculations on slides on the whiteboard. Can pupils read them aloud together? • red + blue = purple • yellow + blue = green • yellow + red = orange Recap that purple, green and orange are secondary colours. They are each made by mixing two of the primary colours together.
Assessment opportunities
• **Through observation:** Can pupils mix two primary colours to create secondary colours? Can pupils paint and print with control? • **Through discussion:** Can pupils talk about the colours they are creating? Can pupils use the term *secondary colour* in context?

Lesson 4

Lesson 4 sees pupils applying the learning from their primary-colour-mixing discoveries to colour-mixing for a purpose: in this session's case, to paint a rainbow. For a more unique outcome, pupils could colour-mix their own secondary-colour palettes to paint a picture of a subject of their own choosing.

▼ **Table 5.4 Exploring colour: Lesson 4**

Objectives
• To use knowledge of primary and secondary colours to mix paint with purpose • To use a brush with control to paint curved lines • To use colour-mixing vocabulary accurately and in context • To know that indigo and violet can be made using different ratios of red and blue
Key vocabulary
red yellow blue primary colour orange green purple secondary colour mix colour wheel line curved arc rainbow indigo violet

Equipment required • Lesson PowerPoint slides • Sketchbooks • Ready-mixed paint in red, yellow and blue • Paintbrushes • Paint palettes
Retrieval and context-setting Show pupils a slide on the whiteboard showing the secondary-colour wheel with the primary colours missing. Can pupils identify where each primary colour should go and explain why? Recap the colour-mixing exploration from the previous session and revisit the colour calculations. In this session, pupils apply their colour-mixing knowledge to the painting of rainbows.
New learning Discuss rainbows with the class. Who has seen one before? Can anybody explain what they are? Rainbows are multicoloured arcs that form in the sky when the sunlight shines through the rain. There are seven colours in the rainbow: red, orange, yellow, green, blue, indigo and violet. Look at the colours with the class and ask the following questions: • Which of these colours are primary colours and which are secondary? • Which primary colour is missing from this list of colour names? (purple) • Can anybody spot any colours that are similar to the missing primary colour? (indigo and violet) These colours are called *indigo* and *violet*. Violet is a purple made by mixing more red than blue, creating a red purple. Indigo is a purple made by mixing more blue than red, creating a blue purple. When mixing these colours with pupils, use 2/3 red and 1/3 blue for violet, and 2/3 blue and 1/3 red for indigo.

Pupil discovery and application

In this lesson, pupils apply their colour-mixing knowledge to paint their own rainbows using paintbrushes and ready-mixed paint. Display a slide showing the rainbow colour order throughout this part of the session for pupils who may need reminding of this.

Set up the classroom for painting. Cover the tables and ask pupils to put aprons on. Each table will need ready-mixed paint in red, blue and yellow; paint palettes; paintbrushes; and pots of water. Each pupil will need their sketchbook open on its next double page. Before painting, ask pupils to draw arc shapes in the air with their fingers. Draw small ones, middle-sized ones and big ones. During this activity, reinforce the notion that arcs are curved lines, not straight lines. In this session, pupils are going to be painting curved lines to form arcs.

Model first painting a red arc, curving from the bottom lefthand side of a sketchbook, up, over and back down to the bottom righthand side. This forms the top of a rainbow. Next, mix an orange paint (using red and yellow) and paint an arc underneath the red so that they touch. Use yellow paint for the next arc, again making sure the top of it touches the bottom of the orange arc. Continue painting arcs to complete a rainbow. If you are using the same paintbrush for each arc, make sure to wash it to avoid unwanted colour-mixing. Blotting the paintbrush with tissue will stop excess water mixing in with the paint and diluting its consistency.

Reflection time

Talk to pupils about their rainbows. What are they proud of? Did they find any aspect of the creative process tricky in this session? What could they do next time to make it easier?

Sing ‘I can sing a rainbow’ with the class. What do they notice about the colours in the song? Are there any rainbow colours missing? Are there any extra ones added in? Are they in the correct order? Sing the song again, changing the lyrics to ‘I can *paint* a rainbow’!

Assessment opportunities

- **Through observation:** Can pupils use paintbrushes to paint curved lines with some accuracy? Can pupils identify which primary colours they need to mix to create each secondary colour? Can pupils mix paint with some control using brushes and palettes?
- **Through discussion:** Can pupils articulate the colour-mixing process using accurate vocabulary? Can pupils describe the shape of a rainbow?

Lesson 5

In this next lesson, pupils begin to understand that the colours they have been learning about over the last few sessions can be described as *warm* or *cool*.

Table 5.5 Exploring colour: Lesson 5

Objectives • To know that colours can be described as *warm* or *cool* (*hot* or *cold*) • To know that colours can be associated with different feelings and emotions • To describe and sort collections of colours • To discuss relevant artworks in terms of the colours used by the artists
Key vocabulary red yellow blue primary colour orange green secondary colour mix colour wheel hot cold warm cool
Equipment required • Lesson PowerPoint slides • Sketchbooks • Ready-mixed paint in red, yellow and blue • Paintbrushes • Crayons, pencils, pens and / or oil pastels in the primary and secondary colours • Paint palettes
Retrieval and context-setting Show pupils slides of colour wheels on the whiteboard. Have some correct colour wheels, and some where the colours are in the wrong places. Ask pupils to look really closely at each. Have the colours been placed in the correct segments? Can they explain which colours need to change places and why? Explain that, today, pupils are going to begin to understand that colours, as well as being described as *primary* or *secondary*, can also be described as *warm* or *cool*. What do they think that could mean?

New learning

Colours can be described as *warm* or *cool*, *hot* or *cold*. The secondary-colour wheel can be split in half to show the warm colours and the cool colours. Show this to pupils on the whiteboard.

Ask pupils to close their eyes and imagine they are somewhere warm, maybe in front of a cosy fire. What colours do they think of? Red, yellow and orange are warm or hot colours. They make people think of sunshine, heat and feeling happy.

Ask pupils to close their eyes again and, this time, to imagine they are somewhere cool, maybe on a snowy mountain or by an icy lake. What colours do they think of this time? Blue, green and purple are cool or cold colours that make people think of winter water and feeling sad. Sometimes people say they are feeling blue, which means they are unhappy.

Artists may use warm or cool colours in their artworks for many reasons. Some choose colours to show how they feel when they create an artwork, or to try to make viewers feel a certain way when they look at it.

Pupil discovery and application

In this lesson, pupils explore warm and cool colours in their sketchbooks, creating collections of each and making links between their new knowledge of warm and cool colours with their understanding of the colour wheel.

Set up the classroom for painting. Cover the tables and ask pupils to put aprons on. Each table will need ready-mixed paint in red, blue and yellow; paint palettes; paintbrushes; a printout of the colour wheel; pots of water and crayons or felt-tips in red, blue, yellow, green, orange and purple. Each pupil will need their sketchbook open on its next double page.

Ask pupils to label one page with the title 'warm colours' and the other page 'cool colours'. They may wish to write these titles in warm and cool colours too! Ask them to fold the colour wheel in half and stick it in the centre of their sketchbook page with the warm colours side (red, orange, yellow) on the warm page and the cool colours side (blue, green, purple) on the cool page. Pupils may fill the rest of each page with mark-making of their choice using different media (paint, felt-tips, crayons, pencils); warm colours on the warm page and cool colours on the cool page.

Encourage pupils to think of words they associate with each collection of colours (such as hot, heat, sun, fire, burn, flame, water, ice, winter, cold, chilly, freeze) and to share their thoughts and feelings with peers. Ask them to write these words on each page – these could be written in warm and cool colours too.

Reflection time
Show pupils some colours on the whiteboard and ask them to tell a classmate whether each is a warm or a cool colour. Do they agree with each other?
Assessment opportunities
• **Through observation:** Can pupils mix secondary-colour paints from primary-colour paints? Can pupils sort colours into warm and cool collections? • **Through discussion:** Can pupils discuss warm and cool colour collections? Can pupils discuss the use of warm and cool colours in relevant artworks? Can pupils discuss the feelings and emotions linked to certain colours?

Lesson 6

This final lesson is classed as an optional extra. Teachers may choose to take the sixth week in the sequence to focus on any misconceptions that have arisen, finish off explorations and artwork not completed or carry out this session. Lesson 6 reinforces the learning from the previous five weeks.

▼ **Table 5.6 Exploring colour: Lesson 6**

Objectives
• To know that colours can be categorised as primary, secondary, warm or cool • To describe, find and sort collections of colours • To compose a flat-lay photograph • To use a tablet or camera to photograph colour collections
Key vocabulary
red yellow blue primary colour orange green purple secondary colour colour wheel warm cool camera photograph photographer flat lay
Equipment required
• Lesson PowerPoint slides • Tablet or camera • Paper or card to use as a photograph base • Objects from the environment to sort into colour collections

Retrieval and context-setting Show some collections of colours on the whiteboard. Can pupils recognise how they have been sorted? **1** Primary colours **2** Warm colours **3** Secondary colours **4** Colours of the rainbow **5** Cool colours In this session, pupils are going to choose a sorting criteria from this list, collect coloured objects that fit the category, then compose and take photographs of them. They are going to be photographers!
New learning Begin this session by discussing what photography is and what a photographer does. • Photography is the art of capturing an image (picture) using a camera. • A photographer is a person who takes photographs. The word *photography* derives from two Greek words meaning 'drawing' and 'light', so it translates as 'drawing with light'. Some people take photographs as a hobby, some take them to capture memories and some people take photographs as part of their job. Show some examples of photographs on the whiteboard. There are many different types of photography – landscape, portrait, macro and astro are just a few! Pupils are going to take a type of photograph called a *flat lay* in this session. A flat-lay photograph is an image taken from above. It is a bird's-eye view. Pupils need to imagine the camera lens is a bird's eye looking down on the world. Pupils will need to be shown how to capture a photograph using the equipment available to them.

Pupil discovery and application

In this lesson, pupils are photographers, creating flat-lay photographs on colour themes. They will apply their knowledge of colour collections to choose objects to place in their compositions. Pupils should play about with different layouts for a flat-lay photograph, decide on their favourite composition and capture it using photography equipment.

This session works well if pupils are placed in pairs or groups. This gives them the chance to discuss composition ideas with each other. Each pair or group will need a tablet or camera to take their photographs with. They also need access to paper or card to create a flat-lay background or base and objects to choose from to place in their pictures.

Start by showing pupils how to use the photography equipment. They will need to know how to zoom in, zoom out and capture a photograph. Outline the task to them and show them outcome examples for inspiration. The pairs or groups need to decide on a theme before they start planning and collecting. They need to create a base for their composition using paper or card (keeping with their colour theme) before they start building their picture. An area of about 1 square metre gives a good amount of space to work in. Once they have created the base, pupils should collect objects that fit their colour theme and place them on their base. Once happy with the composition, pupils should photograph it from above. Once captured, the image may be cropped to ensure the whole focus is the flat lay with no surrounding distractions.

Reflection time

Pupils should look at their photographs and discuss the session with their partner or group. What did they find easy or tricky? If they were to create another flat-lay photograph, what would they do differently? Do they have any ideas for further flat-lay compositions? Maybe they could create one linked to learning in another curriculum area.

Assessment opportunities

- **Through observation:** Can pupils use the photography equipment independently? Can pupils select objects to fit the chosen colour-collection theme?
- **Through discussion:** Can pupils discuss different colour collections using accurate vocabulary? Can pupils talk about their photograph compositions?

Summary

The formats of your own sequences will look different, of course. They'll depend on your year group, your school's curriculum and the artists, media and outcomes you decide to study. But the principle is the same. Successful planning requires that each lesson connects logically to the one before it and prepares the ground for the one to come, and that each sequence allows you to push pupils' practical, theoretical and disciplinary knowledge forwards.

Once you've planned a sequence, you need to consider emphasis. Of all this content, what is the essential learning that every pupil must take away? What is the rich detail and surrounding material that brings this core learning to life? The difference between these two kinds of content – core and hinterland – is the subject of the next chapter.

Further reading

Cherry, P. (2021) *Making Every Primary Lesson Count: Six Principles to Support Great Teaching and Learning*. Carmarthen: Crown House Publishing.

Sherrington, T. and Caviglioli, O. (2020) *Teaching Walkthrus: Five-step Guides to Instructional Coaching*. Woodbridge: John Catt Educational.

CHAPTER 6
CORE AND HINTERLAND

Christine Counsell (2018) argues that, despite the word's suggestion of something subsidiary, the hinterland of a curriculum is 'as important as what is deemed core'.

Core

The core aspects of the art and design curriculum are discussed in Chapters 1 and 4 of this book ('Big Ideas' and 'Age Progression'). They are the essential components – the knowledge, skills and concepts – that pupils are required to know and remember as they journey through their primary education. To ensure they are able to do this, schools sequence core content in small steps to avoid cognitive overload and to ensure pupils deepen their knowledge, understanding and application of it as artists.

In art and design, the core can be placed into three main categories:

- The elements of art
- Skills and techniques
- Artists and artworks.

Within each category lie a number of smaller categories. Taking 'the elements of art' as an example, pupils need to learn the knowledge associated with each – line, shape, space, texture, form, colour and pattern. Thinking about 'skills and techniques', pupils need to learn those associated with different art disciplines, tools and materials. Pupils also need to learn about artists, artworks and art movements.

Hinterland

In high-quality art and design curricula, this core doesn't sit alone; it partners with the concept of the hinterland to deliver meaning to pupils. The hinterland brings the core to life, adding reality and engagement, enrichment and relevance to the classroom experience. The hinterland in art encompasses stories, case studies, examples, visits and visitors, all putting learning into context and connecting the subject to the wider world. While these aspects enhance the core, they play more of a role than simply making it more exciting. They are essential parts of the learning process and help pupils to make sense of concepts they have been introduced to and to develop an appreciation of the subject as a whole.

To illustrate concepts, techniques and styles, teachers could tell stories to bring each to life and help pupils understand. Doing so makes the learning more memorable and hence more likely to stick. For example, when learning to use their sketchbooks, hearing stories of how artists use theirs helps illustrate their purpose in an engaging and relevant manner.

Artist case studies and artwork examples work in the same way. Georgia O'Keeffe and Paul Cézanne illustrate mastery in the use of watercolours; Alma Thomas' work demonstrates a bold use of colour; and the paintings of Miro, Kandinsky and Mondrian show what is meant by abstract art, for example. Pupils could study the lives and works of these artists, how their styles developed over time and how they may have influenced later artists.

Core and hinterland links

Table 6.1 shows how the core and hinterland can link together in the classroom. Those responsible for curriculum-planning and lesson design need to ensure both are thought about and interlinked effectively. The hinterland isn't simply an add-on; it's a thread that should be woven in and out of the core.

Table 6.1 Core and hinterland links

Core content	Suggestions of hinterland scenery
Learning different shading techniques such as hatching, cross-hatching, stippling, scribbling (KS1 or KS2, depending on curriculum design)	Show pupils how artists apply different shading techniques by sharing artwork such as that of Kelvin Okafor, Barbara Walker or Curtis Holder. Watch videos that show them at work, visit their websites and tell stories about their practice, such as how Kelvin Okafor spends over 500 hours on each of his hyperreal portraits or how Curtis Holder won Sky Arts Portrait Artist of the Year in 2020. Use vocabulary to discuss and analyse their artworks.

Core content	Suggestions of hinterland scenery
Beginning to develop an understanding of the element of line (KS1)	Share the quotation from artist Paul Klee that 'a line is a dot that went for a walk', and what that could mean. Look at lines in different artworks, such as the contour line-drawings of Picasso, the Op Art of Bridget Riley or the energetic, abstract works of Wassily Kandinsky, and discuss them. Go on a line hunt and spot different lines inside and outside the classroom.
Developing an awareness of architecture and the role of an architect (KS2)	Look at buildings in the local area, find out when they were built and discuss their architectural features. Find a building with a story in the same village / town / city as the school and explore when it was built, for example the Clock Tower in Leicester, which was built in 1868 and designed by a local architect named Joseph Goddard who won a competition to do so. Invite a local architect to speak to pupils or visit their offices; link this to creative careers.
Learning about the work of artists such as 'Sunflowers' (1888) by Vincent van Gogh	As well as knowing who an artwork is by, the tools and media an artist used and where it sits in the timeline of art history, tell stories and facts linked to it, such as how van Gogh wanted to be known as the painter of sunflowers and that there are fingerprints in some of the paint, indicating that van Gogh must have picked it up while it was still wet. He painted the flowers to decorate his guest room in Arles for a visit by fellow artist Paul Gauguin. Bring sunflowers into class, let pupils smell them, touch them and feel them, before creating representations of them from observation like van Gogh did.
Learning about 'great' artists in history, such as Jackson Pollock and his action painting	Pollock is well known for his action painting, creating large canvases using his drip technique. Wow pupils with the fact that he wasn't the first to do so and that he took inspiration from the lesser-known Ukrainian-born artist Janet Sobel. Show photographs and videos of Pollock at work to show the scale he worked at and how he transferred the paint from his brush to the canvas in an unconventional manner. Painters don't have to apply paint carefully to paper using a brush.

Core content	Suggestions of hinterland scenery
Learning about portraiture as an artistic representation of a person	As well as teaching pupils about the proportions of the face and how to draw a portrait or self-portrait, show them examples of portraits of different faces from different times and places. Share famous portraits, such as those created by Picasso, van Gogh and Frida Kahlo, but also by lesser-known artists such as Amoako Boafo, who paints the skin of his subjects with his fingers, or Matt Small, who creates mosaic portraits using debris such as discarded metal. Think about the role portraiture plays in informing us of the appearance of important figures in history. Visit a gallery, museum, castle or stately home to view portraits in the real world.

Choosing hinterland

Curating hinterland well takes the same care and attention as curating core content; the most effective hinterland I've seen is shaped by answering four questions that a teacher might ask of any piece of potential content:

1 **Does it bring the core to life?**

The point of hinterland is to help core knowledge stick, so the first question to ask of a potential addition is whether it illuminates the concept being taught. A story about Pollock's drip technique has its place in a unit about action painting; the same story would be out of place in a unit on observational drawing. If core and hinterland aren't aligned, the lesson will lack focus.

2 **Does it speak to this class, this year, this school?**

Schools' contexts and their pupils' lives are different. The same core content can be supported by very different hinterland. A Norfolk class studying colour might find hinterland in local marine artists and the changing colour of seas; an inner-city Birmingham class might find it in the Bullring's shopfronts nearby. Both are good. Neither would resonate in the other school.

3 **Does it broaden, or does it narrow?**

Teachers should consider the implications of the 'Visualise' report findings shared in Chapter 3. Hinterland that defaults to the same names year after year will reinforce a narrow canon even as your core content is solid. Conscious hinterland choices have a powerful impact on inclusion.

4 Is it accurate?

I include this question last even though it should really be a precondition of anything you include in your curriculum. Hinterland founded on questionable attribution or remembered-slightly-wrong anecdotes risks more than a missed educational opportunity; it can leave pupils misinformed. When in doubt, look it up.

In the spirit of building up a repertoire, teachers could start a 'hinterland bank' habitually. For example, you could create a Google Doc, split by core topic, of artists, anecdotes, examples and ideas for visits and visitors. Over time, it will build into a rich resource that tells you what brings each element of the curriculum to life for pupils in your care.

Summary

Core and hinterland are not adversaries, but allies in curriculum design. The core provides pupils with the knowledge, skills and concepts they require to grow as artists; the hinterland provides them with reasons to care about that knowledge; ways to remember it and understand it; and a sense of how it connects to the wider world of art they are joining.

Too much core and not enough hinterland leaves pupils who can recite the elements of art but cannot explain why any of it matters.

Too much hinterland and not enough core leaves pupils who have heard a lot of great stories but do not have the technical wherewithal to make art of their own.

This chapter has described how core and hinterland work together; the next chapter discusses some of the difficult concepts and common misconceptions that cause pupils difficulty along the way and suggests some strategies for helping pupils through these trouble spots.

Further reading

Counsell, C. 'The Dignity of the Thing' on Christine Counsell's blog [online] Available at: https://thedignityofthethingblog.wordpress.com (Accessed: 16 May 2026).

Myatt, M. (2018) *The Curriculum: Gallimaufry to Coherence*. Woodbridge: John Catt Educational.

Van Gogh Museum 'Five fascinating facts: Van Gogh's Sunflowers' [online] Available at: www.vangoghmuseum.nl/en/art-and-stories/stories/all-stories/5-things-you-need-to-know-about-van-goghs-sunflowers (Accessed: 16 May 2026).

CHAPTER 7
DIFFICULT CONCEPTS AND MISCONCEPTIONS

Art and design is one of those subjects in which many teachers feel they lack the adequate subject knowledge and skills to teach effectively. The All-Party Parliamentary Group for Art, Craft and Design Education's 'Art Now' inquiry (2023) found significant gaps in subject expertise across the primary workforce, with the report concluding that the deficit in primary initial teacher education for art and design urgently needs addressing. The worries many teachers have can be calmed, reduced and even eliminated through targeted subject-specific CPD, improved disciplinary understanding and a change of mindset.

Difficult concepts

The elements of art

The elements of art are mentioned in the key stage 1 descriptor from the national curriculum: 'pupils should be taught to develop a wide range of art and design techniques in using colour, pattern, texture, line, shape, form and space' (DfE, 2013). It is useful to think of these elements as the building blocks of art. They are the components used by artists when creating artwork.

Colour

In primary school, pupils learn about primary, secondary and tertiary colours; the colour wheel; tints, tones and shades; complementary and harmonious colours; contrasting colours; the way colours make them feel; and more.

Pattern

Patterns in art are created using shapes, colours, symmetry and repetition. Patterns are all around, whether natural, such as butterfly symmetry, or human-made, such as the fabric design of a dress.

Texture

Texture can be classified in two ways: actual or implied. *Actual texture* is the way something feels if you were to reach out and touch it.

Implied texture is a visual representation; artists use different skills and techniques to create textural illusion in their work.

Line

The phrase often attributed to Paul Klee, that 'a line is a dot that went for a walk', captures the idea well for young pupils. Artists use many different types of line, such as straight, curved and wavy.

Shape

Shapes can be described as *geometric* or *organic*. Geometric shapes are those more commonly recognised by pupils, such as squares, rectangles, circles and triangles. Organic shapes are irregular shapes.

Form

A form is three-dimensional. It has height, width and depth; forms include cubes, cuboids and pyramids. Artists give two-dimensional artworks the illusion of form through the use of different techniques.

Space

Artists create a sense of space in their artwork using lines and shapes. There are two types of space: *positive* (the object) and *negative* (the area around the object). Space creates depth and perspective in a composition by creating a foreground, middle ground and background.

It is important that pupils are introduced to these elements early on through the units of work and sequences of learning they experience. Teaching these building blocks helps pupils develop their individual artistic skills and their understanding of how artists create art.

Colour theory

Colour theory refers to the way colours mix, harmonise and contrast with each other. It was first written about by Leone Battista Alberti in 1435. In primary school, pupils should develop an understanding of the colour wheel; primary, secondary and tertiary colours; warm and cool colours; and complementary and contrasting colours. When teaching the secondary-colour wheel, it is important to be really explicit about where the colours sit. A colour sits between the two colours that mix to make it. Orange sits between red and yellow; green sits between yellow and blue; and purple sits between blue and red.

Tints, tones and shades

These words are often used interchangeably but, when talking about mixing different tints, tones and shades with paint, they mean different things. In the following statements, *hue* refers to the base colour before it has anything added to it.

- A tint is created when white is added to a base hue.
- A tone is created when black and white (grey) are added to a base hue.
- A shade is created when black is added to a base hue.

Close looking

Pupils need to be taught to slow down and look closely at the world around them. Close looking is sometimes called *slow looking*. When carrying out observational drawing or painting, it is important that pupils understand that they are creating their own visual representation of what they can actually see. Encouraging pupils to look, then draw, look, then draw, look, then draw until they have completed their artwork helps to reinforce this understanding.

The benefits of close, sustained looking are well documented in arts-education research. Tishman (2017) describes slow looking as a deliberate practice that develops pupils' powers of observation, patience and aesthetic discernment, with knock-on effects for thinking across the curriculum.

Subject-specific terminology

It is important for teachers to use accurate, rich and ambitious subject-specific vocabulary with their pupils, and this can be tricky for those with gaps in their knowledge of art. There are places to turn for support, such as the NSEAD website, which has a glossary of terms that support the national curriculum for art and design. When planning out units of work, the key vocabulary should be explored and noted so that teacher confidence is high when using it and pupils learn confidence with it too. Meanings of words should be explicitly taught, and understanding checked to avoid misconceptions. See the following two examples for vocabulary used correctly and incorrectly by pupils in the classroom.

- Pupil A: 'I've created an abstract representation of the four seasons.' This pupil used subject-specific vocabulary accurately and in context. They had made fluid marks on their canvas in browns, oranges and greens. They explained which part of their painting represented winter (dark brown), spring (light green), summer (bright green) and autumn (orange).

- Pupil B: 'I've drawn a portrait of a tree.' This pupil had picked up subject-specific vocabulary but was using it in the wrong context. They knew that the word 'portrait' referred to the subject of an artwork. They had misunderstood that the subject, in the case of a portrait, is a person.

The research on tier-two academic vocabulary (Beck, McKeown and Kucan, 2013) shows that pupils acquire subject-specific terms most effectively when they encounter them in meaningful context, are taught their meanings explicitly and have repeated opportunities to use them in talk and writing. The art and design classroom offers all three conditions naturally, provided teachers plan for the vocabulary deliberately rather than hoping pupils will absorb it.

Pupils need to be able to talk about their own work and the work of others using this language. They are required to discuss technique; artistic choices; meanings and messages in artwork; and personal preferences. Many schools find it useful to create word mats with key vocabulary on them to scaffold talk and writing in art. Words associated with each element of art can be grouped together for ease. The following lists provide some of the basic vocabulary associated with each, but are by no means exhaustive:

- **Colour:** primary, secondary, tertiary, warm, cool, pale, bright, vibrant, rich, deep, bold, subtle, complementary, contrasting, pastel, pure, hue, shade, tint
- **Pattern:** repeat, regular, irregular, symmetrical, tessellating, natural, geometric, striped, rotating, linear
- **Texture:** actual, implied, rough, smooth, bumpy, soft, hard, hairy, glossy, matt, wet, dry, gritty, uneven
- **Line:** straight, curved, long, short, thick, thin, dotted, diagonal, horizontal, vertical, continuous, parallel
- **Shape:** regular, irregular, geometric, symmetrical, two-dimensional, three-dimensional, natural, abstract, square, rectangular, circular, triangular
- **Form:** natural, human-made, cuboid, conical, spherical, cylindrical, height, length, width, depth
- **Space:** big, large, small, open, enclosed, narrow, wide, high, low

Misconceptions

Art and design is the same as design and technology

Having the word 'design' in the name of both subjects can and does cause confusion. For a project to be considered a true design and technology project, there must be a product, a user and a purpose in mind. Designing and making a coat for a dog to wear in the rain is an example of a DT project because it has a product (the coat), a user (the dog) and a purpose (to protect it from the rain). Art and design is not the same as design and technology.

Art is an easy option

There is still a common mistaken belief in society that art is easy, but this is not the case. It is a highly skilled and technical subject and should be treated as such. To be successful in art, pupils need to do far more than colouring in. They need to develop and refine technical skills, think creatively, think critically, learn about the practice of other artists, understand art history, and so much more. Raising the profile of the subject in schools helps erase the stigma attached to it.

Teachers can just turn up and teach art

This misconception follows on from the previous one. Art is not an easy option, and teaching and learning in the subject requires as much thought and preparation as any other on the curriculum. Sequences of learning and individual lessons need to be carefully planned out, building on previous learning and providing a pathway to develop small steps of progression, to explore, to experiment and to discover.

There are also the resources to consider here. Art and design lessons need to be thought about way in advance of teaching them. Rooting around in cupboards at the last minute to find resources is not conducive to a smooth-running, high-quality teaching-and-learning experience, especially when the materials and tools cannot be found. Regular audits and clear organisation of resources in schools help reduce the prospect of this happening, as does planning and preparation in advance from class teachers. Teachers cannot just turn up and teach art.

Artists wear berets

Yes, this is true: some artists may well wear berets. But the reference here is to the stereotypical imagery that surrounds the notion of being an artist. This may seem a ridiculous statement to make, but there are so many stereotypes still floating around that it seems a valid one to include in this section. Web searches for images of artists bring back numerous hits of smiling individuals wearing aprons, covered in paint, holding paintbrushes and standing at easels. Icon searches on popular presentation-software packages show artists in berets, holding paint palettes and brushes. Both illustrate a very narrow view of what an artist is and what an artist looks like.

Teachers and schools can counter these stereotypes by ensuring pupils see images of, and learn about, a wide range of artists with visible and invisible differences.

Art must be beautiful

A misconception that many adults and children have is the idea that art equals beauty. Of course, many artworks are beautiful, such as Claude Monet's 'Water Lilies' (1920) or Edgar Degas' 'Little Dancer Aged Fourteen' (1880), but it is more accurate to think of art as being a communicator. It does communicate beauty, but also many other messages and emotions. Think of Picasso's 'The Old Guitarist' (1903–04), which evokes sadness, the figure hunched over with a solemn face and sorrowful blue colour palette. Art speaks, and sometimes what it says can be deeply moving and sometimes even uncomfortable.

Art is also used in protest and to push for social change. When used for this purpose, it can be extremely powerful. *The Artivist* (2023) by Nikkolas Smith, published by Penguin Random House, is an effective way to share this concept with pupils.

Art must be perfect

The misconception that art must be perfect can make pupils freeze in fear before they even begin. It is the misconception that drives the eraser-led drawing, the screwed-up paper, the 'I can't do it'. Pupils need to understand that art is not about perfection. It is about expression and creativity, which can take any number of forms. The work in a sketchbook is a record of trying things out, of making mistakes, of changing direction. The fear of getting it wrong is the very thing that stops pupils making real progress as artists. The job of the primary teacher is to build a classroom culture in which pupils are released from the burden of perfection and given permission to play.

Primary teachers need to have art and design qualifications

In most cases, primary teachers have the tricky task of teaching all the subjects on the curriculum. It is unrealistic to think every teacher has a GCSE, A-level or degree in every subject they teach. The phrases 'I'm rubbish at art' or 'I can't draw' can often be heard from the mouths of teachers – teachers whose experiences of art at school clearly did not give them the belief in themselves as artists.

However, when it comes to teaching primary-school art and design, the passion and enthusiasm for the subject are of paramount importance. Skills and knowledge are great, but getting pupils excited about a subject is priceless, and qualifications are not needed for that. Teachers struggling with their confidence can rehearse the skills they are going to teach pupils, or source videos to help them. Using a teacher sketchbook is a way that they can learn and practise alongside pupils too.

Only 'famous' artists should be on the curriculum

No, no, no. How does an artist get to such a celebrity status that they become famous? It is so hard to quantify, and really quite unnecessary in this context. Yes, pupils need to learn about the artists who have shaped art as it is today, the ones who dominate the history books, but schools need to inspire pupils with more than this Eurocentric canon of art history (see also Chapter 3 on the 'Visualise' report findings).

Relevant artists need to be on the curriculum: artists who enhance the acquisition of knowledge and skills and inspire pupils in the classroom, whether they create artwork that sells for six figures or they are a local graphic designer who lives in a bungalow 100 feet from the school gates. Just because an artist does not have national or international recognition does not mean their work is not of a high quality. A curriculum should be more than only 'famous' artists.

Cheaper materials are just as good

Tight school budgets mean teachers are encouraged to cut back wherever possible when it comes to resources, but art and design is a subject that just does not work without equipment and materials. It obviously pays to shop around for good deals when sourcing such materials, but it is important to remember that cheaper does not always mean better.

Opting for the lower price can mean quality is greatly reduced, and the cost saving is actually a false economy: think glue sticks that do not stick, sketchbook covers falling off after only one art lesson and brushes that shed more bristles than they keep. With sketchbooks in particular, you really do get what you pay for in terms of paper quality. They need to withstand both wet and dry media, so it is important the paper thickness and absorbency are suitable.

A writing pencil will do

The marks made with a writing pencil are not the same as those made with sketching pencils, which are specifically designed for drawing. The numbers and letters on the pencils tell you their hardness or softness. *H* stands for 'hard', and *B* stands for 'black'. Hard pencils create lighter marks, and soft pencils make darker marks. The numbers on the side of pencils relate to this level of hardness or softness. A 6B pencil is softer and darker than a 2B pencil. Likewise, an 8H pencil is harder and lighter than a 2H.

Here is a list of pencils from lightest to darkest and hardest to softest: 9H, 8H, 7H, 6H, 5H, 4H, 3H, 2H, H, HB, B, 2B, 3B, 4B, 5B, 6B, 7B, 8B, 9B.

Sketching pencils enable artists to create a greater range of tones and textures in their work. A writing pencil (or HB) simply will not do the same job as a range of sketching pencils.

Only draw in a sketchbook

Believe it or not, there are actually teachers and leaders in schools who preach this to their school communities. A lack of subject understanding causes this rather deep misconception. The dictionary does not help here either, describing a sketchbook along the lines of a large pad of paper for sketching on; and neither does the *sketch* part of the word itself. On the contrary, sketchbooks are for a lot more than just drawing. They can be used for painting, collage, recording research, scrapbooking, and more. As for the tools and media used on their pages, anything and everything can be tried out. Sketchbooks are places to explore and experiment, to take ideas on a journey and to make discoveries. Sketchbooks are art books, art journals; they show a pupil's artistic development over time.

Summary

All the misconceptions mentioned in this chapter will be recognisable to any primary teacher who has taught art and design for any length of time. They are not fixed, and they certainly do not have to dent our confidence to teach the subject. Armed with clarity, correct vocabulary and a classroom atmosphere where pupils feel comfortable getting things wrong, the difficult concepts become teachable, and the misconceptions can start to be unravelled.

The following chapter tackles the practical issue of how much teacher modelling and how much pupil exploration there should be in the primary-art classroom, drawing on Tom Sherrington's distinction between Mode A and Mode B teaching to address the question.

Further reading

All-Party Parliamentary Group for Art, Craft and Design Education (2023) 'Art Now: An Inquiry into the State of Art and Design teaching in Early Years Foundation Stage, Primary and Secondary Education' [online] Available at: www.nsead.org/community-activism/policy-andresearch/all-party-parliamentary-group (Accessed: 16 May 2026).

Beck, I.L., McKeown, M.G. and Kucan, L. (2013) *Bringing Words to Life: Robust Vocabulary Instruction*. New York: Guilford Press.

DfE (2013) 'Art and design programmes of study: key stages 1 and 2' [online] Available at: https://assets.publishing.service.gov.uk/media/5a7ba810ed915d4147621ca0/PRIMARY_national_curriculum_-_Art_and_design.pdf (Accessed: 16 May 2026).

Smith, N. (2023) *The Artivist*. London: Penguin Random House.

CHAPTER 8
MODE A AND MODE B

In *The Learning Rainforest* (2017), Tom Sherrington discusses Mode A and Mode B teaching, having earlier developed the concept on his Teacherhead blog. Mode A is teacher-led lesson design; Mode B is a more exploratory approach for pupils. The two modes can be summarised as follows:

- **Mode A** involves teachers explaining new content, modelling how to do something, giving pupils opportunities to practise, checking for understanding through feedback and assessing retention through testing.
- **Mode B** involves pupils exploring and discovering, working hands-on with materials, encountering content that is striking or awe-inducing, working on open-ended projects and exercising choice in what they make.

Individual lessons do not have to be one or the other, but a careful curation of methods from either or both. It is useful to think of these as the pick-and-mix of teaching, or the one from the top, two from the bottom choice of numbers on *Countdown*.

Instead of being a random selection, teachers need to select the most appropriate methods to suit the intended learning in their classrooms. Some lessons will require more from Mode A, others Mode B, but a carefully curated blend of both over time will lead to optimum learning. Sherrington has suggested that, for many subjects, the balance might lean significantly towards Mode A, with Mode B occupying a smaller proportion of classroom time. But it is important to note that this is not intended as a one-size-fits-all approach. Considerations need to be made regarding individual cohorts, pupil needs, objectives of a lesson and the disciplinary aspects of a subject. Due to its nature, teaching and learning in art and design feature a much heavier percentage in the direction of Mode B.

Sherrington's framework sits alongside a wider body of research showing the value of explicit, teacher-led instruction. Hattie's (2009) meta-analysis of over 800 studies on classroom influences identifies teacher clarity, direct instruction and feedback among the highest-impact approaches in education, all of which sit comfortably within Mode A.

Mode A

What does Mode A look like in the primary-art classroom, and when might teachers choose to use the approaches within it?

Teacher explanations and modelling are both of extreme importance when teaching new skills and techniques. Pupils need to be explicitly taught certain aspects of the art and design curriculum. Hatching, cross-hatching, stippling with pencils, blending with oil pastels, scoring and slipping with clay are all examples of the many techniques that pupils need to be shown how to do before they independently apply them to their own artistic practice. Precise teacher instruction is required: a mixture of clear oral explanation alongside the modelling of the practical element of a technique in small, scaffolded steps. Teaching these techniques in isolation helps the early formation and acquisition of them.

Taking hatching and cross-hatching with a sketching pencil as the example here, the teacher would need to:

- show the pencil to pupils and tell them what grade it is
- activate pupils' prior knowledge of these pencils
- activate any prior knowledge pupils have of sketching techniques
- demonstrate hatching by actually doing it: model the process in front of pupils first, drawing a series of parallel lines in any direction but not touching – the closer they are together, the darker the shading effect; this can be shown by drawing several examples to illustrate
- repeat the previous step with cross-hatching: this technique involves hatching again, but with parallel lines in different directions, so the hatching crosses – as before, the closer the lines are together, the darker the shading effect.

At this stage of lesson delivery, pupils need to be able to hear the teacher and see what they are doing clearly. They must have an uninterrupted view of the teacher's hands. This can be ensured through effective use of a visualiser to cast the teacher's actions onto the whiteboard, via a prerecorded video or by pupils standing around a table to watch. An important consideration with the latter is that pupils will be watching the teacher's actions from awkward angles, maybe even upside down, depending on their positioning around the desk. This may affect their grasp of the technique being demonstrated. Teachers must check pupil understanding before they independently apply their learning. This can be done through careful questioning both during and following demonstration.

As well as demonstrating the practical side of the art experience, teachers may also model the thinking processes of an artist: talking through their thoughts as they create, modelling how to activate a growth mindset when 'mistakes' happen and verbalising decision-making.

Following on from the modelling stage, pupils need to be given the opportunity to apply and deliberately practise what they have been taught independently. In the previous example, pupils would try out hatching and cross-hatching in their sketchbooks, perhaps creating tonal bars using the technique or drawing an object of their choice and then applying the shading techniques to it. At this point, the teacher may circulate the class, observing, listening in to conversations and questioning to check understanding and level of mastery of the technique that has been taught. Through this, the teacher can give immediate, in-the-moment feedback to move learning forwards.

Mode A approaches also suit the delivery of subject-specific knowledge in the art classroom. Direct explanation and teacher instruction ensure pupils are fed the required knowledge to succeed. Such knowledge could relate to artists, artworks, art history, art movements, or could be connected to media or tools. Acquisition of this knowledge may be tested through direct questioning or quizzes.

This approach to lesson design leads to more convergent outcomes from pupils in their art lessons, with teachers prescribing the intended activity, processes and outcomes. Examples of such activities include the rehearsal of specific painting or drawing techniques, following particular steps to create a piece of artwork or imitating an artist's style.

Mode B

What does Mode B look like in the primary-art classroom, and when might teachers choose to use the approaches within it?

Art and design is a creative subject. As such, pupils need to be allowed a large amount of the subject's dedicated classroom time to create in. They need the opportunity to explore, experiment and discover through inspiring, meaningful experiences. They need time to immerse themselves in their imaginations, to play with resources and to communicate visually in their own unique way. Art is hands-on;

it is doing, making and creating. Art as a discipline is a Mode B subject at heart.

Art gets messy, and this can put practitioners off the freer approach to learning that comes with Mode B teaching in the subject. But through play and exploration, pupils discover. They develop their own styles, find out which resources work for them, discover their likes and dislikes, their strengths and weaknesses, and find their artistic characters in the classroom. Without the opportunity to do this, there is the potential for pupils to end up as carbon copies of each other as artists, all producing work that looks and feels the same.

Experiences that allow pupils to explore and discover still need careful thought and preparation. Setups need to be purposeful and with learning intentions in mind. For example, prior to using charcoal to draw a landscape or portrait, pupils would benefit from the opportunity to play with the medium, discovering its fragility, its smudging and blending abilities, the amount of pressure needed to create light and dark tones, and more. This could be done in sketchbooks, on scrap paper or any canvas, just as long as pupils can play with no restrictions or expectations. When using new media or tools for the first time, pupils benefit from having this time to explore.

When teaching about different artists and artworks, teachers are not only delivering subject knowledge to pupils, but also presenting them with inspiration, awe and wonder. Pupils can use and apply these ideas in their own work. The still-life works of Henri Matisse, Vincent van Gogh and Frida Kahlo can give pupils food for thought when it comes to creating their own. The art classroom is not a place for pupils just to copy the work of relevant artists, but rather to take them as a stimulus to discover their own style in the genre.

If looking at Matisse's 'Goldfish' (1912) or 'Still Life with Geraniums' (1910), rather than attempting to copy the paintings accurately frame by frame, pupils may create their own still-life compositions, collecting and arranging their objects, thinking about the background and the table they sit on before choosing the media to create a visual representation of the scene. They are then painting what they can see, not what the artist being used as inspiration saw. They are developing and using their own creativity, not imitating someone else's.

When working in sketchbooks, pupils can be given autonomy over how they present their work, choosing where and how to place a title, whether to prepare a background, how to compose their pages, where to draw, write and place pictures. The Year 5 artist-research sample lesson plan in Chapter 9 explores this concept further. Sketchbooks should be as unique as the pupils they belong to, so choice in how they are used is key.

Discovery in action

On a rainy day, a group of EYFS pupils, dressed in puddle suits and welly boots, were given the opportunity to play with colour mixing. Pots of red, blue and yellow powder paint were placed on a table outside, under a shelter, alongside a variety of containers, spoons and brushes. The pupils structured their own play, scooping the powder out of the pots with the containers and transporting it to puddles to mix with rainwater to create their paint. Using classroom paintbrushes, large decorator brushes and toothbrushes, they mixed the powder and water together. In true EYFS style, this play developed and, rather than using one colour paint, pupils decided to mix two. The screams of excitement were a joy to hear when they found that mixing two created a third colour. Shouts of 'I've made orange' and 'the blue and yellow have turned the puddle green' could be heard all around the playground. The pupils fed off each other's discoveries to further their own. The playground and its puddles became more and more colourful, and eventually the pupils noticed that the puddles had turned brown.

What did this play teach them about colour theory?

- Mixing two colours can create a third colour.
- Red and yellow make orange.
- Yellow and blue make green.
- Red and blue make purple.
- Mixing red, yellow and blue makes brown.

Essentially, the pupils were making discoveries about primary and secondary colours. With teacher intervention in the play, they would also learn these terms.

The outcomes from Mode B teaching and learning approaches are divergent in nature. Pupils have choice over their work, whether in terms of subject matter, skills or techniques applied, the colours used or choice of media. Therefore, the artwork differs around the classroom and each piece reflects the ideas and creativity of the individual that created it.

Summary

The art experience in primary schools needs to be a careful balance of the structured teaching of skills and techniques (Mode A) and open-ended, creative exploration (Mode B). An effective marrying of the two approaches helps develop confident, curious, unique artists with a bank of skills and knowledge to draw on and apply to their own practice.

Further reading

Cherry, P. (2021) *Making Every Primary Lesson Count: Six Principles to Support Great Teaching and Learning*. Carmarthen: Crown House Publishing.

Rosenshine, B. (2012) 'Principles of instruction: Research-based strategies that all teachers should know' in *American Educator*, 36(1), pp.12–19, 39.

Sherrington, T. 'Teacherhead' [online] Available at: https://teacherhead.com (Accessed: 17 May 2026).

Sherrington, T. (2017) *The Learning Rainforest*. Woodbridge: John Catt Educational.

Sherrington, T. and Caviglioli, O. (2020) *Teaching Walkthrus: Five-step Guides to Instructional Coaching*. Woodbridge: John Catt Educational.

CHAPTER 9
SAMPLE LESSONS

Many educators have tried to develop a model for a typical art lesson sequence, the intention being to help non-specialists plan and deliver art lessons that include key components required for optimum learning. But the subject doesn't fit into the box of uniformity that other subjects do.

A structured approach starting with retrieval, followed by instruction, guided practice and then independent application lesson by lesson, is suited to many subjects and indeed some art sessions, but most definitely not all. Cognitive-load research suggests that the same approach can become counter-productive as pupils gain expertise (Kalyuga et al., 2003). Teachers and pupils benefit from the freedom to vary lesson design based on the knowledge and skills being taught and the desired learning outcomes.

There is no right, wrong or expected way to structure the delivery of the elements of a lesson in art, as long as choices are well thought through and offer pupils experiences to aid their continuous development and deepening understanding. One good art lesson can look completely different from another good art lesson, both equally successful in meeting the needs of their pupils.

Art is not only a place for skills and technique; it is an exploratory subject. Pupils need time to be in the moment, present with tools and media and given free rein to explore, experiment and discover for themselves. It is important to consider this when planning lessons. Exploration is fundamental in the development of skills and an essential in art education.

Early Years teachers are experts when it comes to this approach, giving their pupils ownership of their own learning and discoveries. This can make less experienced teachers feel 'out of control' of a lesson; this freedom given to pupils being an alien notion when compared to other curriculum areas. But it is an essential element of an art learning journey. Freedom doesn't need to mean chaos; when conditions for learning and attitudes of pupils are positive, understanding can be deepened, and meaningful links made. The opposite of chaos ensues, and a calm, engaged and purposeful atmosphere created.

When planning a lesson, it's important to consider the aim of the session, to unpick the proposed learning and decide on the best approach to deliver it to pupils. The following suggested lessons could be used in your classroom.

Taking a dot for a walk with Year 1

This session is part of a sequence, with pupils already having discussed lines, using the Paul Klee quotation as stimulus: 'a line is a dot that went for a walk'. Pupils have previously taken dots for different walks in their sketchbooks using a variety of mark-making media and created collages from straight lines.

Objectives

- To find lines in the environment
- To describe a variety of lines
- To draw a variety of line types

Key vocabulary

dot line straight curved long short thick thin curved wavy loopy zigzag horizontal vertical diagonal

Equipment required

- Line-hunt sheets (see Figure 9.1) or sketchbooks
- Clipboards
- Tablet or other photo-taking device (optional)
- Pencils
- Rulers
- Chalk
- Black A4 sugar paper
- 'Blau' by Wassily Kandinsky (1922)

Indoor Line Hunt

Find a	✓	Draw the lines you have found
straight line		
curved line		
long line		
short line		

Find a	✓	Draw the lines you have found
zigzag line		
wavy line		
thick line		
thin line		

▲ **Figure 9.1 An example line-hunt sheet for assessing line types inside; the same questions can be asked for lines outside**

Retrieval and context-setting

In the previous session, pupils explored straight lines. Ask whether anyone can remember the way they were described. A straight line is a line travelling in one direction without any curves. Can anyone spot any straight lines in the classroom?

Explain that, in this session, the focus is on more than just straight lines. The class are going to be line hunters and will be finding and describing lines in their indoor and outdoor environments. They will then draw as many different lines as they can. They will be using black sugar paper, chalk and charcoal to create their line art.

New learning (direct instruction)

Lines are all round us. So far in this sequence, pupils have described lines as long, short, straight, thick, thin, curved, wavy, zigzag and loopy. There are three new words to introduce in this session: *horizontal*, *vertical* and *diagonal* – these are words that can be used to describe lines too:

- A horizontal line travels from left to right, like a horizon.
- A vertical line travels up and down.
- A diagonal line joins two corners of a square or rectangle but is not an edge.

Show an example of each on the whiteboard as simple lines, then examples of each in the real world: Use a photo of a house to show vertical and horizontal lines on the windows, door and bricks. A triangular roof, a side view of a playground slide or a ladder leaning up against a wall can all be used to illustrate diagonal lines.

Ask pupils whether they can spot any examples of these line types in the classroom and to discuss them with a partner.

Pupil discovery and application

In this lesson, pupils carry out two activities: a line hunt and a line draw. If time doesn't allow for both, pick one of the two.

Activity 1: We're going on a line hunt

Give pupils copies of line-hunt sheets (or they can record directly into their sketchbooks), clipboards and pencils. Explain that they are going on a line hunt to try to find lines in the environment. You may wish to explore both the indoors and outdoors or just focus on one. The sheet should specify the line to find, have a space to tick when it is found and a box for pupils to draw the lines in. Once completed, these sheets can be stuck in sketchbooks. You may wish to plant some objects before the lesson to ensure pupils can find all the line types!

Optional extra: Take photos with tablets or other photography equipment.

Activity 2: Drawing lines using chalk on black paper

For this activity, pupils need black sugar paper and white chalk. Allow them the opportunity to fill the paper how they want using as many of the line types they have been learning about as they would like to. Some may want to use rulers to draw their straight lines, but this is not essential: they may draw them freehand if they wish. Let pupils choose.

Reflection time

Show the class the abstract painting 'Blau' (1922) by Wassily Kandinsky. Ask pupils to talk with a partner about what they see. Can they describe the lines? Can they use the new vocabulary introduced in this session? Where are the diagonal lines? How many diagonal lines can they see? Can they spot any horizontal or vertical lines? Pupils may need you to draw their focus to the shape at the bottom with the lines criss-crossed over it to see examples of these.

Assessment opportunities

- **Through observation:** Can pupils identify lines in the environment? Can pupils draw different types of lines?
- **Through discussion:** Can pupils describe the lines they find in the environment? Can pupils talk about horizontal, diagonal and vertical lines?

Exploring charcoal with Year 2

In this session, pupils explore the medium of charcoal. Some may have previous experience of using the medium in EYFS or Year 1; others may not. If they haven't, it would be advisable to give them a chance to explore and play with it in a session before this one, or at the beginning of this lesson. The charcoal and paper could be put out on their tables at the beginning of the lesson for them to pick up, feel and mark-make with before the 'new learning / direct instruction' element of the session takes place.

It's useful for teachers to be aware that:

- charcoal snaps easily – communicate this to pupils so that they are aware before they get upset that they have broken it!
- charcoal creates a lot of dust – blowing it off the paper prevents any unwanted smudging
- charcoal is messy – hands do get covered in black dust
- charcoal needs a fixative, otherwise it will rub off the surface it has been drawn on.

Objectives

- To experiment with charcoal
- To begin to control marks made with charcoal
- To produce textures and patterns

Key vocabulary

charcoal line mark texture pattern hatch
cross-hatch scribble smudge pressure tone light
dark dust rub tip side mix blend

Equipment required

- Sketchbooks
- Rubbers
- Pots of water
- Charcoal
- Paintbrushes
- Chalk

Retrieval and context-setting

Have a discussion with pupils about drawing. What does the word 'drawing' mean? What can we draw with? List any mark-making tools and media pupils come up with, such as pencils, pens, pastels. Recall any previous drawing experiences they may have had both at school and home. Explain that, today, pupils are going to draw with charcoal, one of the oldest drawing materials in the world. Charcoal sticks are burned pieces of wood that can be used like pencils to draw marks and make lines.

New learning

Show pupils some examples of artwork created using charcoal to engage and inspire. Start with early cave paintings, through to the charcoal drawings of Edgar Degas and on to the modern-day urban landscapes of Stuart Jarvis. Demonstrate some different ways marks can be made using the charcoal. This could either be a prerecorded demonstration video played on the whiteboard or a live demonstration using a visualiser or with pupils watching around a table.

Explain that the way we use charcoal can produce different textures and patterns on paper. Show pupils how to hatch, cross-hatch and scumble with the charcoal, how changing the pressure we apply as we draw changes the tone of the mark made, how rubbers can be used to rub away the charcoal and how fingers or a blending stump can smudge the marks made. Finally, explain to pupils that other media can be mixed with charcoal to create different effects. In this session, they have access to chalk and water to mix and play with alongside the charcoal.

Pupil discovery and application

Give pupils their sketchbooks, charcoal, chalk and access to water and paintbrushes. Give them time to explore the techniques demonstrated and also to try out anything else with the charcoal on a double page in their books. They may also explore blending the chalk and water and the charcoal and water.

Reflection time

In pairs or groups, ask pupils to discuss their experiences with the charcoal. What did they discover? How did mark-making with charcoal compare with drawing with pencil? What happened when they mixed the charcoal with the water? What would they like to try next?

Assessment opportunities

- **Through observation:** Can pupils make a variety of marks with the charcoal? Can pupils lead their own explorations?
- **Through discussion:** Can pupils describe the marks they make? Can pupils discuss how it feels to work with the charcoal?

Creating a paper sculpture with Year 3

Pupils will already have had some experience with sculpture in KS1. They should be aware of what a sculpture is, that a person who makes a sculpture is called a *sculptor* and be able to share their ideas, experiences and imagination through this medium.

Objectives

- To turn paper from 2D into 3D form
- To join pieces of paper together to create width, depth and height

Key vocabulary

sculpt   sculpture   sculptor   2D   3D   form
bend   fold   scrunch   roll   curl   cut   stick
join   fix   width   depth   height

Equipment required

- A variety of paper types and colours
- Glue
- Scissors
- A3 or A4 card or paper to use as a base

Retrieval and context-setting

Show three different artworks on the whiteboard: one painting, one drawing and one sculpture. Ask pupils to point to the sculpture. How do they know it is a sculpture? A sculpture is 3D artwork. Remind the class of the last time they created a sculpture. Do they remember it had depth, height and width? What does this mean? In this session, they are going to create another sculpture, this time out of paper.

Before embarking on the teacher-directed aspect of the lesson, give pupils a chance to play with paper. Give them some scrap paper and challenge them to turn it from 2D to 3D form. They can discuss their ideas with their peers and explore the paper's sculptural capabilities.

New learning

Allow pupils the opportunity to share the ways they turned their paper from 2D to 3D, then show them some other techniques. Show them how it can be scrunched, folded, curled, bent and looped. Demonstrate how two or more pieces can be joined together, either by looping through each other like a paper chain or with glue, to create taller or wider structures.

Pupil discovery and application

Give pupils a base of A3 or A4 card or thick paper, then let them sculpt! Give them a variety of paper types in a variety of colours, along with scissors and glue, and let them use their imaginations to create their paper sculptures. Invite pupils to give their finished sculptures a name.

Reflection time

How did pupils find the paper-sculpting process? Was there anything they found challenging? Is there anything they would do differently if they were to make their sculptures again? Is there anything they would like to add to their finished pieces?

Display all the sculptures together to create a gallery. Invite visitors from other classes to come and admire the work.

Assessment opportunities

Through observation: Can pupils use scissors accurately to cut the paper? Can pupils turn the paper from 2D to 3D form? Can pupils join two pieces of paper intentionally and accurately?

Stepping into a painting with Year 4

This session can be carried out with any year group, but the level of questioning and artwork chosen to explore and 'read' will need to be age appropriate and relevant to the pupils in the class. Any artwork can be used for this activity. Whole sessions can be spent discussing and responding to artwork through dance, drama or music or a task can be given to pupils to carry out in their sketchbooks. In this session, pupils read the painting 'The Football Players' (1908) by Henri Rousseau.

Objectives

- To use visual literacy skills to *read* an artwork
- To be able to describe some of the key ideas and techniques used by an artist
- To learn about the work of a relevant artist

Key vocabulary

look notice read see hear smell feel touch
composition colour line space technique materials
figures foreground middle ground background

Equipment required

- 'The Football Players' (1908) and 'Tiger in a Tropical Storm' (1891) both by Henri Rousseau, displayed on the whiteboard, tablets or other photography equipment
- Sketchbooks
- Drawing / painting materials
- Cards each showing either eyes, nose, ears or hands for the discussion activity
- Balls for the freeze-frame activity

Retrieval and context-setting

Talk to pupils about artworks they may have studied during their previous years in school. Can they remember who they were by, what the subject of them was and how they were created? Explain that, today, they are going to explore a painting by a famous artist named Henri Rousseau. Has anyone heard of this artist before? Display 'Tiger in a Tropical Storm' (1891) and ask whether anyone recognises it. This is one of Henri Rousseau's paintings, but this session's focus is on a different one, called 'The Football Players' (1908).

New learning: guided discussion of the painting

Display the painting of 'The Football Players' on the whiteboard and give pupils a few minutes to look at it in silence. Explain that they are looking slowly and closely at the painting to take in the details. What is happening? Then ask them to share with the person next to them something they have seen.

Next, have a discussion as a class. Think about the composition of the painting: what can pupils see in the foreground, middle ground and background? What do they notice first in the painting? Why do they think this is? Can they see any shapes and patterns? What colours has Rousseau used? Are they primary or secondary? Warm or cool?

Then focus attention on the figures in the painting. What are they doing? Are they still or moving? How has Rousseau shown this? Do they look happy? Look at the expressions on their faces and decide. How has Henri Rousseau made it look like his footballers are having fun?

Pupil discovery and application

In this part of the session, pupils are to work in groups of four to explore the painting further; firstly, with a discussion, followed by a drama activity.

Activity 1: Discussion

Give pupils four cards: one with eyes on, one with a nose on, one with ears on, one with hands on. These cards are to act as prompts for the senses: sight, smell, hearing and touch. Pupils should imagine they have stepped inside the painting. Taking a card at a time, they are to use their senses to explore. So, when they have the card with eyes on, ask them to envisage what they can see all around them. They are to think about looking up, down, left and right. Repeat for the other senses.

Activity 2: Freeze-frames

Pupils are to look closely at the painting; in particular, the figures. Each pupil is going to take on the role of one of them. Pupils each need to look at their figure's body positioning and the expression on their face and then become them. Each group of four pupils should create a freeze-frame of the painting that is photographed by the teacher. The only prop given to each group is a ball.

Reflection time

Do pupils like the painting? Ask them to give reasons for their answers. If they like it, why do they like it? Is it Rousseau's use of colour, his choice of subject, the figures in the painting? If they don't like it, ask them to justify why. Does it remind them of any other artwork they have seen?

Assessment opportunities

Through discussion: Listen in to pupil conversations about the painting. Are they able to discuss elements of it?

Artist research with Year 5

While the subject of art is a creative, practical one, there are times when pupils are required to write. However, the expectations of writing in art and design are different from those of the other subjects on the curriculum. Art's expectations are more succinct, with short phrases; adverbs and adjectives to convey artistic technique; pupil likes and dislikes; reflections and facts. This session is one where pupils carry out a mixture of both writing and artistic creation as they fill a double-page spread in their sketchbooks with an artist study. The artist in question in this lesson is Alma Thomas, but the structure can be used for any artist.

Prior to this session, allow pupils time to prepare the 'ground' in their sketchbooks; that is, breaking up the white space of a double page. They may wash it with paint, add brushstrokes, rip and stick down pieces of paper – it's up to them. This can be a quick 10-minute session, but needs to be done in advance so that paint or glue can dry. This not only adds to the visual appeal of the finished pages, but also helps those pupils who may be reluctant to start when faced with two blank pages at the beginning of a lesson.

Objectives

- To learn about the life and works of a relevant artist (Alma Thomas)
- To take inspiration from sources to develop their work
- To use a sketchbook as a space to record research, explore and note down thoughts and feelings, likes and dislikes

Key vocabulary

research Alma Thomas artist abstract acrylic paint
concentric circles pattern vibrant colours bold colours
nature mosaic brushstrokes rhythm repeating shapes
vertical lines stripes dashes bird's-eye view or perspective
Washington Colour School racial segregation

Equipment required

- Sketchbooks
- Tablets / laptops
- Art resources such as paint, pencils, pastels, pens, paintbrushes

Retrieval and context-setting

Recap the artists the class have already studied in previous years. Can they remember the names of them? Can they recall any of their artworks? Did they like or dislike their work? Why? Did these artists inspire their own development in terms of technique and style? In what way?

New learning

Prepare some slides documenting key events from Alma Thomas' life to share with pupils. Talk through them one at a time, giving pupils the opportunity to ask questions throughout. Explain that Alma was influenced by nature; share some of her work. Her work is abstract. Can pupils guess what inspired each painting? Paintings to share may include 'Autumn Leaves Fluttering in the Breeze' (1973), 'White Daisies Rhapsody' (1973), 'Sky Light' (1973), 'Iris, Tulips, Jonquils and Crocuses' (1969), 'Snoopy Sees Earth Wrapped in Sunset' (1970) and 'The Eclipse' (1970).

What do pupils notice about her style and technique? Draw their attention to the dash brushstrokes that have a mosaic-like appearance. How could the colours she used be described? They are bright, bold and vibrant. Alma painted patterns and often painted concentric circles or bird's-eye views. She was part of the Washington Colour School movement.

Pupil discovery and application

Pupils should fill a double-page spread inspired by Alma Thomas in their sketchbooks. They can write a heading wherever they choose and in whichever style they want to. They can include key facts and dates shared during the teacher direct-instruction part of the session, or they can do some further research for information themselves. As well as writing facts, pupils can have a go at drawing or painting in the style of Alma, creating their own concentric circles or bird's-eye views using mark-making media, collage or paints. They can swatch the colours Alma used, draw a picture of her and express their likes and dislikes.

Reflection time

Ask pupils to leave their sketchbooks open on the tables and to walk round the classroom looking at the work of their peers. Encourage talk as they observe, with pupils sharing similarities and differences between the sketchbooks and recapping the facts they have learned.

Assessment opportunities

- **Through questioning:** Ask pupils some key questions related to the input delivered by the teacher about Alma and her work.
- **Through observation:** Can pupils create their own representations of Alma's concentric-circles bird's-eye views? Can they create dashes with their mark-making media or paintbrushes?

Summary

The five sample lessons in this chapter are stylistically very different from each other. That is intentional. A line-hunt followed by chalk-drawing in Year 1 requires very different choices from a study of Henri Rousseau's work in Year 4 or an artist-research page on Alma Thomas in Year 5. However, what all five lessons do share is a focus on balancing teacher direction with pupil exploration, on being clear about what pupils should know and be able to do at the end of the session and on building reflection and assessment into the lesson.

Each lesson includes one of the most difficult issues for primary-art teachers: assessment. The following chapter deals with this in more detail.

Further reading

AccessArt: Inspiring the Teaching and Learning of Visual Arts [online] Available at: www.accessart.org.uk (Accessed: 16 May 2026).

Kalyuga, S. et al. (2003) 'The expertise reversal effect', *Educational Psychologist*, 38(1), pp.23-31. Available at: https://doi.org/10.1207/S15326985EP3801_4 (Accessed: 15 July 2026).

Smithsonian American Art Museum 'Alma Thomas: Resources for Educators' [online] Available at: https://americanart.si.edu/artist/alma-thomas-4778 (Accessed: 17 May 2026).

CHAPTER 10
ASSESSMENT

Subjectivity

The assessment of primary art and design is a topic that creates much discussion among educators. On one hand, there are the leadership teams requiring quantitative data on the progress of pupils for whole-school assessment systems, and on the other hand there are those fighting for alternative methods of celebrating and recording pupils' abilities and achievements in the subject. Assessment in art is hard! Why? Firstly, because it is so subjective. What one person deems a 'wow' piece of beauty may be an eyesore to another. We all see and like differently.

There is a need to approach assessment in art and design carefully, with a specific purpose in mind and with a clear understanding of its subjective nature. The art world is huge, encompassing a multitude of disciplines, tools and media. Often, artists develop love and expertise in only a few areas of this vast expanse, so to attempt to assess and label a pupil's achievement across the *whole* art spectrum seems out of touch with the subject in the real world. However, summative-data needs in education require teachers to place pupils into a 'best fit' category – notably 'working towards', 'expected' and 'exceeding' expectations. But it is also important to recognise individual pupils' strengths in particular areas.

When assessing pupils as artists, it's important to remember that art is an area of the curriculum where they are encouraged to embrace their individuality and communicate through their own unique creations. For them to do this, they need to feel safe and comfortable during the creative process and be encouraged to explore, experiment and take risks. Unfortunately, the idea of having a work of art marked can thwart this desire and create unnecessary feelings of anxiety in the classroom. So, assessment approaches need to be unobtrusive and seen as *kind*, *specific* and *purposeful* – adjectives taken from Ron Berger and the video-based instructional resource 'Austin's Butterfly' (2012).

Comparing the skills and level of mastery of artists and artwork on any level is an incredibly difficult task. Who is to say Picasso was a greater talent than Kahlo? That van Gogh's portraits are more skilled pieces than

Monet's waterlilies or that Klee's use of colour is superior to O'Keeffe's? It is an impossible task and something that must be considered when trying to pocket pupils into levelled descriptions of achievement. It's also important to consider the enormity of the subject of art – the numerous disciplines, genres, history. An individual may be a phenomenal fine artist but lack creativity; another may have exceptional skills in painting abstract pieces but find it tricky to draw accurately from observation. Both would be considered remarkable artists in their chosen fields but, in school grading systems, where do they fit?

Methods of assessment

This doesn't mean the subject is free from assessment needs; just that a different approach may be more suitable. Indeed, it's essential to know how well pupils are progressing and achieving to develop the next steps in their journey as artists. This is the purpose of assessment. However, labelling pupils as 'on track' for end-of-year expectations is a tricky task. What even are the end-of-year expectations? That there are no national exemplifications for each year group in the subject makes this even harder for teachers. To help with this, many schools create their own standardisation folders for each year group, either photographing or keeping examples of pupils' work across year groups and art disciplines. These can be kept in physical folders or digitally.

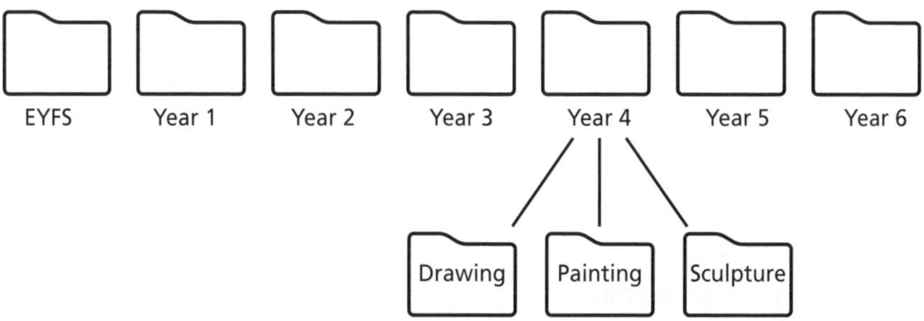

▲ **Figure 10.1 An example digital-folder structure**

To get an all-round picture of a pupil's achievements, there is a lot of information to be considered. As teachers, we need to know that pupils:

- are developing the use of tools and media they have been introduced to
- are developing the artistic processes and techniques they have been taught

- have a developing understanding of how to articulate themselves as artists using subject-specific vocabulary
- are developing a disciplinary understanding of the unique nature of art
- are retaining key knowledge relating to the theoretical aspects of the subject, such as artist names, artworks and art styles.

It is not enough solely to look at the final outcome of a sequence of learning and judge a pupil's artistic prowess on it. Consider that, on occasions, a fabulous piece of artwork can happen by accident. The paint blobs in the right place on the page, or a perfectly positioned line is the result of a jog to the arm. Does this make the pupil a *greater-depth* artist?

Likewise, a pupil who shows a superb mastery of certain skills in their sketchbook then produces an end-of-project piece without demonstrating such ability: does this rank them as only *working towards*? A final piece of work will only ever show a snippet of a pupil's capabilities.

Therefore, alongside it, teachers need to consider a pupil's acquisition of skills over time, their use of subject-specific vocabulary, their retention of relevant knowledge, their understanding of theory, the way they handle different tools and work with different media. It's only by considering all these elements together that a judgement will be a true reflection of a pupil's *overall* ability.

So, which methods can be used to assess primary-school art successfully? There is no one-size-fits-all answer to this; rather, there is a pick-and-mix selection of possible formative (assessment *for* learning) and summative (assessment *of* learning) assessment methods to choose from and combine to suit the needs of teachers, individual cohorts and learning experiences. These include:

- observations of pupils at work
- listening in to peer-to-peer conversations
- teacher–pupil conversations
- questioning and quizzing
- looking at a pupil's sketchbook journey
- the assessment of a final piece.

Observing

Week by week, during art sessions, tune into peer-to-peer conversations and listen out for art talk. Are pupils discussing ideas, techniques and processes? Are they using subject-specific vocabulary? Having a notebook or feedback journal open on your desk to make notes in can be useful. Tune into the objectives of each session when assessing, but also to the wider notion of the subject and what it means to work as an artist. Circulate the classroom and join in with conversations: effective questioning can help you deduce the knowledge and understanding pupils have acquired during the session and retained from previous ones. It will also highlight any gaps that need addressing or revisiting.

▲ **Figure 10.2 Example classroom discussions**

It may sound obvious, but observing pupils at work tells you so much about their artistic abilities. Remember, in art, that the process is just as important as the product when it comes to the development of skills and techniques. Watch how your pupils handle tools and materials, how they apply what they have been taught, how they approach exploration and experimentation. Do they learn from others, draw on what they have seen then add a personal twist to their artwork? Make notes and step in to support development where appropriate. Try to avoid telling pupils what they *should do* but, in conversation, make suggestions for next steps and ask pupils whether they *thought about* trying something different. This adds a more positive twist to feedback, celebrates what they have already achieved and puts pupils in charge of their own journeys.

Sticky notes can be your best friend when assessing art. Make notes of conversations and observations and add them to your feedback journal or stick them into pupil's sketchbooks. They won't deface their work and you can even purchase tracing-paper sticky notes!

The scrutiny of a final piece of artwork can tell you a lot about a pupil as an artist, but it's important to remember it won't tell you everything. If, during a sequence of learning, you want pupils to learn to mix different tints and shades of a colour and then they use them in a final piece, then you can be confident they have achieved that objective. However, looking at a final piece in isolation will not tell you whether that same pupil can articulate the process they went through to obtain those colours, nor will it tell you whether they can use subject-specific vocabulary to describe them. This is why, when assessing artwork, it is so important to do so in a variety of ways.

Recording assessment

Many teachers find it useful to have a dedicated space on their planning documentation to jot down assessment notes. This could be on the medium-term overview or on an individual lesson plan. Boxes with the headings 'working towards', 'expected' and 'exceeding', with space for names and brief notes, help the organisation of assessment. It's not necessary to write the names of the whole class in the boxes; indeed, if pupils don't appear in the 'working towards' or 'exceeding boxes', it can be assumed they are working at the expected level.

A final piece, in collaboration with discussions with its creator, a study of their sketchbook journey and observations of them at work will provide a true all-round picture of them as an artist.

Measuring achievement

When planning to teach units of work, it is important that teachers are clear on what it is they want pupils to achieve. What are the expectations of them during each lesson and what is expected of them by the end of an entire learning sequence? Being specific helps the measuring of achievement and gives both teachers and pupils focus. When organising lessons, it is important to think carefully about this assessment focus – what do teachers want to know and how are they going to find it out? Is it through conversations, observations, a look at outcomes or a mixture of all these approaches? It's also important to think about whether a whole cohort is being assessed or a specific group of pupils. If the latter, it's imperative that pupils are on a rotation so that the same pupils aren't assessed in depth each week and others not at all.

Planning learning objectives

The following planning documentation from the Haringey Education Partnership art curriculum outlines outcomes and learning throughout a complete unit of work. Each individual lesson, however, has more focused and specific learning objectives, such as these taken from Lesson 3:

- To find lines in the environment
- To sort and name collections of lines
- To describe a variety of lines
- To draw a variety of lines

Year 1 Sequence 2 Taking a line for a walk

This sequence of learning takes pupils on a fun exploration of line, one of the basic elements of art!

Sequence Outcomes
Pupils who are secure in this sequence will be able to ...

... understand that 'a line is a dot you take for a walk'
... talk about and describe different lines
... notice and discuss the lines artists have chosen to use in their work
... use tools and media effectively to create different lines
... sort collections of lines
... spot different lines in photographs and their environment
... use lines effectively to draw different shapes
... create an abstract piece of art using lines and shapes
... use line effectively to draw from observation
... use glue with control to create a collage by arranging paper lines on a backing
... understand that a collage is a piece of art made by sticking different materials onto a backing

▲ **Figure 10.3 Planning documentation from the Haringey Education Partnership art curriculum**

Once learning objectives are established, teachers can decide on the best methods to deduce whether individual pupils have met them, and where assessment opportunities will arise during the lesson.

Summary

When deciding on your assessment approach in school, in short, consider the following points:

1. Know your why! Think carefully about why you are assessing. What is the purpose? What is it going to tell you about a pupil and how will you use this information to aid progression? Don't assess for the sake of assessing!

2 Vary your assessment methods – each one is useful in informing you of different aspects of a pupil's artistic persona. Using a variety of methods over time helps build a wider picture of pupils as artists.
3 For the same reasons as point 2, vary the focus of your assessment. Don't just look at particular skills or the retention of art-history facts. Art is bigger than that, and narrowing assessment doesn't do the subject, or your artists, justice.
4 Each pupil's starting point is different; they are all on individual artistic journeys and progress will differ from pupil to pupil.
5 Assessment and feedback go hand in hand. There is no point assessing if you are not going to share findings with pupils. Ron Berger's work on 'Austin's Butterfly' (2012) offers a useful framework: effective feedback should be kind (given respectfully), specific (identifying precisely what could be improved) and helpful (giving the pupil something they can act on). 'The symmetry on the left wing is really effective; the right wing could match it more closely' is feedback a pupil can use; 'lovely picture' is not.
6 Use feedback time as an opportunity to encourage and motivate pupils as artists, to focus positively on next steps and to move learning on.
7 When assessing in the moment, and advising pupils on *next time*, make sure you actually do give them a *next time* to explore in!
8 Art is subjective; it is an expression of an individual's thoughts and feelings. Look at pupils' artwork through understanding and impartial eyes, and don't be swayed by your own artistic preferences.

Case studies

Assessment in art and design: Paul Carney, visual artist, author and educator

On one level, it's very easy to assess art. You simply spread the pupils' work out in front of you; the 'best' work leaps out at you so powerfully that you have to fight the urge to get your camera out right there, while the 'worst' work looms large, its limitations painfully there for all to see. These clear and evident extremes of attainment are apparent to everyone, not least of all the pupils who are doing the actual work. This is their reality. No one wants to be embarrassed and have their work laughed at by their peers – everyone wants praise, to get it right, and to be the best.

This anxious sense of self rarely works the other way round; pupils rarely feel confident they have achieved high standards: unless they are very young, of course, because little ones usually have such a glowing sense of pride in their work at that age. This wonderfully positive stage of life evaporates when children reach a self-critical stage of growth around the age of seven years, but until then it's lovely to see. After that time, it's usual for children (and adults), constantly to look over their shoulder and compare themselves with those they perceive to be the highest attainers. They are their own worst critics. It is this illusion of high attainment that the art teacher is attempting to combat. Good art teachers know how these biases work; they understand the mechanisms of creativity that always assume everyone else's work is better than their own and they work hard to overcome them.

So, what's their secret? How do they get pupils to be kinder to themselves, to enjoy others' work without being judgemental, to understand how critically but fairly to reflect on their own work, to know how to move forwards without fear of failure? Well, good art teachers do not measure attainment; they measure progress, and this is a hugely different assessment objective. When I measure attainment, I reinforce the same negative biases that tell pupils 'Their work is better than mine'. When I measure attainment, I post only the 'best' few pieces of work on social media to get the accolades and likes I crave. When I measure attainment, I emphasise that art can be ranked from best to worst, that those with more skill and ability can 'do' art and those without it can't. Talk to any group of adults in a pub or a café and they will depressingly apply these metrics to themselves, because that's how they were assessed at school or, rather, they weren't properly assessed and so that is their default mode.

When I measure progress, on the other hand, I'm focusing on progress from a starting point, not who has climbed to the highest point on a peak. Let me give you an example. When I'm doing a training course, I might observe that person A is working really hard, they are very engaged, attentive, or astute, while person B appears distracted or distant. I might assume that person B isn't interested in the course and has been sent on it against their will, or perhaps they don't even like art and never wanted to do it in the first place. Of course, this may be true, but rarely do I take account of the circumstances behind their apparent disinterest. Some people have only had to travel a mile or so down the road, while others have been up at the crack of dawn, traversing jammed roads or rail networks over huge distances. Some may have had a terrible night's sleep, had to grapple with getting their screaming kids off to school, or have had their headteacher telling them they want them back at school as soon as the course is over.

There are many hidden factors that affect performance, and it isn't a level playing field. We aren't all starting from the same point. Strangely, in my experience, those who have to put in the most effort to reach their destination usually appreciate it much more than those who find it easy. But, that aside, when we solely measure attainment, we do not take proper account of the things that led to it or hindered it. By measuring progress, we try to take account of the whole learning process, of the underlying factors that contribute to, or affect, that performance. How do we do that?

Well, all teachers are familiar with planning lessons and units of work. They devise curriculum content and progression maps to plan out what pupils will know and do at key points in their development, usually conveniently arranged in year group or termly chunks. The art of good planning is getting these end points just right for all; high enough to be challenging, yet not so high as to be unobtainable. Planning is vital, but it is only a means to an end; it isn't the end itself. Planning is like a speaker writing their speech in advance. It doesn't imply that the speech itself is going to go exactly the way it was intended. Many factors can affect what is said and how it's delivered and, even then, the speaker cannot be sure how the speech was received and, more importantly, what was learned and remembered from it. We, as teachers, don't have the luxury speakers have. We cannot simply let our pupils walk out the classroom not knowing what they learned. We need to be as fully aware as we can be of what pupils know, understand and remember of our lessons. Yet, we don't have the time or resources to inspect, test or appraise every pupil learning individually.

The best tool we have to monitor pupils' learning and understanding is formative assessment. Formative assessment is an ongoing, dynamic, fluid process of teacher and pupil interaction that is used to modify teaching and learning activities to improve attainment. It should be a collaborative, shared experience; a series of one-to-one, peer or whole-class dialogues, not a series of authoritative judgements passed down from the teacher to the pupil. Assessment in art is not a marking process, where teachers inform pupils of what they got right or wrong, because there aren't any right and wrong answers. In more formal learning situations, of course, art teachers can correct misuse of language, spelling, grammar or even application of skills, techniques and processes. This is desirable and, where teachers don't have confidence in skills themselves, they should practise practical tasks themselves in advance of the lesson, or reference video instructions for guidance. Preferably, these videos are demonstration videos the school have purchased in advance or have created themselves.

During the formative-assessment process, in real time, the teacher acts as a shepherd, guiding, nudging and steering pupils to specific intentions using judicious feedback, rather than barking commands and issuing binary yes / no, right / wrong responses. The most effective feedback for pupils is when their successes and strengths are recognised, the progress they have made is highlighted and the areas they could improve are indicated, supported by specific, actionable advice. This whole experience should use positive, motivational language, because we do not want the assessment process to hinder future learning. Art and creativity, perhaps more than most other subjects, is dependent on the pupil wanting to keep trying. This is because learning skills takes considerable practice, but also because it is an optional subject and, in any case, anxiety is especially high when we are creative, for reasons I mentioned earlier.

I've adapted five general feedback strategies set out by Dylan Wiliam to meet the needs of the art classroom. They are:

1 **Set learning intentions that are clear and structured,** but not so rigid that they do not allow for personal, creative interpretation. For example, I might demonstrate how to paint a watercolour wash but there's no reason why pupils couldn't be given the freedom to select their own colour combinations when practising. You can use WAGOLLs to provide clear examples of what success looks like, but don't over-rely on them, especially in art and design, because pupils may just copy them, and they take away individual creative responses.
2 **Use the classroom critique method to appraise performance.** The art crit, where we gather everyone around the work we have produced and discuss it, is a time-honoured technique for improving performance and appraising the learning that has taken place. It involves whole-class discussions and learning conversations around pupils' creative outcomes; to reflect on the experiences of what has been produced, both emotionally and practically; to provide platforms for dialogue, discourse and support about future learning routes. Pupils are excellent at giving constructive advice, providing support and encouragement, so use crits liberally and often, both during and at the end of work.

3 **Provide feedback that moves the pupil forwards.** There is an important distinction to be made here. Good assessment should focus on improving the learner not the learning – developing the person not the product. An example of this would be when we are teaching art techniques. We don't tell the pupil they are doing something wrong (emphasising the learning) but show them how to improve (emphasising the learner). There are many feedback techniques, however. My favourite is the Praise Sandwich. This is where we begin a learning conversation with positive praise, then add judicious areas for improvement that are specific and actionable, and then leave with praise: 'This is good, Samina. I love how you have used colour here. Just be mindful of those untidy edges here and there or you won't be able to recognise the shape. But, other than that, it's really great work.' If you don't have the expertise to provide specific feedback, then you have to rely on the classroom critique method instead, where advice and feedback is given collaboratively.

4 **Facilitate pupils as resources for each other,** building on the classroom crit method; you might use pair work or small-group peer assessment. This is where pupils could drill down into other pupils' work and give really insightful feedback. It's a great strategy to swap one table's work with another and let them study it to provide feedback along guidelines you've set out for them. They love doing it and are very shrewd judges – only make sure they are fully aware of the criteria they are assessing to.

5 **Activating pupils as owners of their own learning.** Pupils need to be able to assess themselves fairly and understand how best they can move forwards to improve. This involves increased levels of metacognition – what they know about their learning and what they do about it. These are cycles of thought and action, and they are happening all the time when we make art. We consider what we are going to do, we act and make something, then reflect on the outcome or process. These reflections inform our next cycle or, in the worst cases, hinder it completely, where we give up out of frustration. Being able to make fair and reasonable judgements about the art we make, both as we are doing it and after we have completed it, are crucial to being a successful artist.

I'd also add a final point, and that is that you need to provide opportunities to action the advice that has been given or there's not much point giving it! To do this, allow follow-up time in future lessons or in form time, then check the progress again (or get pupils' peers to do it for you). Make it clear that some aspects of learning take considerable time to master; they can't be learned in one, two or even three lessons. Show pupils how some artists spend a lifetime learning things and still aren't satisfied with their results. Resilience, growth mindset and delayed gratification are all important aspects of the creative process.

Another important aspect of being creative is learning how to be fair, honest and unemotional about criticism and advice. Many pupils go to pieces if they don't get the praise they are looking for, or if the advice is spoken harshly. It's not their fault here. They are so eager to do well and please you. Often, praise is so limited in their lives, and it brings them validation and emotional security. Building a growth mindset can really help here – the belief that a person's capacities and talents can be improved over time. I did this all the time in the art room, by explaining to pupils that they aren't competing with each other; that mistakes are an important part of learning; that they aren't trying to make exact copies of things; that they can only ever hope to do their version of something, not make it perfect. All these aspects of creativity are ongoing and occurring all the time, so I made positive reinforcement posters and put them up in the room, then referred to them when I needed to. It's a huge part of building confident, creative learners.

Starting points

There is another important aspect to assessment in art, however, and that is measuring starting points. You can't measure progress until you know your pupils' general ability in several areas of art: skills, knowledge and creativity. I developed a simple exercise to do this that takes about an hour to do, and I would do it at the beginning of each year:

Skills and creativity assessment for EYFS or KS1 pupils
Show the class a photograph that is an imaginary starting point for a drawing. I like to show a mysterious door in a forest and ask: 'Draw what you think is behind this door.' It could be a doorway into another world or favourite place or person. Lead pupils into possible ideas, but don't give them answers or let them copy. I inform them that I will be looking for original, imaginative ideas and also how well they can describe their idea using drawing. When the drawings are complete, I assess their ability to realise their ideas through drawing – their fine-motor skills and their level of imagination.

Skills and creativity assessment for KS2 pupils

I give each pupil a small junk object collected from my shed or my oddment drawer in the kitchen: objects such as screws, bottle tops, curtain hooks and keys are excellent. I ask pupils to make a drawing from observation of this object in around 15 to 20 minutes. I inform them that I want them to draw the object as accurately as they can, in the correct proportions and, if possible, adding shading. Next, I ask them to transform their drawing into an imaginary picture. I say they can rotate it, add things to it, make it into a scene or a character or even just an abstract pattern. I inform them I am going to be looking at their ability to come up with novel, original ideas. This is an adaptation of a Torrance Test, which is the standard way of measuring creativity. I'm looking for the level of their drawing skills and their level of imagination.

That is my baseline assessment complete! Note that you can simply look at pupils' sketchbooks or folders from the previous year if it's easier. You may also have transitionary data and summative reports from previous years that can all be used to assess the starting points across all three areas. Some teachers tell me they do a portrait project each year to assess pupils' starting points, but all this does is tell you how good they are at drawing faces. It doesn't give you other essential information about literacy or creativity.

Next, I get everyone into a circle or group, and we celebrate and enjoy our pictures, commenting on what is most interesting and successful. As the teacher, I am looking for distinct assessment areas here. I can choose to share this information with the class or not, but I want to measure drawing ability in terms of the level of skill, attention to detail or successful transference of their idea and their level of original, imaginative thinking. I make judgements about their work to the three assessment strands of 'working towards', 'working at' or 'working at a greater depth', where 'working at' is the expected standard of drawing for their age and being able to describe an idea that few other people have thought of in the room. It takes about an hour to do the assessment and discuss / assess it in the group, but this now gives me three measurements of ability:

1. Pupils' general drawing ability, described as 'working towards', 'working at' or 'working at a greater depth'
2. Pupils' level of creative imagination, described as 'working towards', 'working at' or 'working at a greater depth'
3. Pupils' ability to access and describe their own and others' artworks using verbal and written communication.

What you should find from doing this is that some pupils are very skilful at drawing, but not so imaginative. Some are imaginative but not so skilful and some are literate and articulate but not imaginative or skilful. In our current art-education climate, it is usually the skilful ones who receive the most recognition, rather than the budding art critic or most imaginative ones.

Endpoints

There should be clear endpoints that pupils are working towards. In my curriculum planning, I devise a set of descriptors that outline endpoints at significant stages so that staff and visitors can be sure that pupils are making good progress in the subject. For example, by the end of KS1, I want most pupils to know and recite their primary and secondary colours, to be able to hold and use a pencil and a paintbrush with accuracy and precision, to know the names and key features of artists' work we have looked at, and so on. In this way, assessment is much easier to implement, and it should be visible for both pupils and staff to ensure everyone knows what achievement looks like.

Assessment should be inclusive

There are two other strands of assessment to mention: pupils with special educational needs or disabilities (SEND) and those who are very talented at art, who are described as having Higher Learning Potential (HLP). These are complex, separate subjects in their own right, but they still need consideration when making formative classroom assessments.

Essentially, if a pupil flies through your lesson easily and still achieves a very high standard of outcome, then your lesson has clearly been too easy for them. The national curriculum advises that you should provide challenges and, if required, extension activities related to the same topic, rather than moving them on to something new. To do this, you need to raise the bar. You might even need extra specialist help and support to develop distinct activities for these pupils, in which case they can't take part in your whole-class dialogue when assessing them. Either way, it's important to outline to the whole group where this higher attainment lies in relation to expected standards. If it is well above the level for this age, then it will be counter-productive if everyone else compares their art to it. You can diffuse this somewhat by making this clear to the rest of the group, but it doesn't always work. In any event, teaching HLP pupils of art requires you to design projects that have more open outcomes rather than teacher-led tasks.

This works in the opposite direction too. Some pupils with SEND may not be able to access your lesson in typical ways and so may need supporting materials, usually in the form of adapted handouts or some other means. Now, we shouldn't be lowering standards for these pupils, or setting different types of work, because the expected intention is that work for pupils with SEND should be ambitious and the same as the mainstream lesson. However, there are numerous times when adaptive teaching and specialist prior preparation is unavoidable. When assessing art, I would make allowances for pupils with SEND where I felt it was appropriate. More often than not, in mainstream settings, pupils with SEND aren't overly hindered when making art, because it isn't as reliant on literacy and numeracy as other subjects. If I felt that it would be counter-productive or harmful to include a pupil with SEND in a whole-class crit, either because their work wasn't the same as the others' or it would affect their confidence, I'd adapt the way in which I involved their work in any crit. In all cases, I'm attempting to avoid making any pupil feel excluded in the best way possible, so as to preserve their motivation.

Some forms of assessment are more visible than others

The most important form of assessment you do is the formative dialogue in the classroom. However, assessment isn't just a grade on a piece of work, it's also those stickers you give out, the rewards for the best work; it's your comments and casual conversations, prizes or certificates in assembly; it's even your body language. Your pupils are seeking approval; they are watching everything you do! 'I didn't get a certificate', 'I didn't get my work on the wall', and so on. When walking around a room, you can't praise everyone's work or you'd sound silly, so tell the group that if you walk past their work and say nothing it means that they are doing well, and you don't feel they need any help. This way, your silence is a positive action. Use a thumbs-up sign or tell a whole table you are going to check their work, have a look, then say: 'Excellent work, well done.'

Your assessments should be reliable, replicable and accurate

Standardise your assessment and keep it consistent. You can't make meaningful measurements if the nature of them keeps changing. You will not get consistent results if one class have to do their assessment exercise on the last Friday afternoon before Christmas break and the other did it on a relaxed morning in Spring. It won't have much meaning if you entered some data based on your gut feeling about your class when you were overly tired, and other, comparable data after studying their sketchbooks and folders for an hour when feeling refreshed. Don't put all your eggs in one basket. Important decisions can't be made on one small piece of evidence. Make meaningful judgements based on evidence over time. Also, it's not easy to do, but you have to remove bias. You may have a pupil whose behaviour is very challenging or who is particularly disruptive or challenging to teach, but this should not affect your assessment of their work.

Feedback should be efficient and effective

Assessment is the best classroom tool you have for improvement, and it should be a positive, informative, class-based experience that gives pupils clear direction for their next steps. If there is any writing to be done, it should be done by the pupil themselves, perhaps in their sketchbooks so you can monitor it later, because all feedback or assessment advice should be followed up on by the pupil. Pupils should be allowed time to act on the advice given, and this follow-up work should be checked by the teacher to ensure it is happening correctly. This might be as simple as looking over the shoulder while they are doing the follow-up work and giving them a word of encouragement; it doesn't have to be additional written assessment.

Take your verbal feedback-given stamps and throw them in the bin – or make art from them. If senior leaders want to see evidence of pupils receiving feedback and acting on it, look at the pupils' work – all the evidence is there! Read the pupils' own feedback statements about their performance, which should contain evidence of assessment dialogue being received and acted upon. Then look at the work itself. Can you see anywhere where the pupils have received advice from the teacher then worked on it? Make it a target for pupils to have to show *you* they have done this – not the other way round, where teachers have to evidence 30 examples per class. How can they show *you* they have practised shading neatly since you gave them the feedback? How might they show *you* they have researched the artist you asked them to? Flip the expectation to provide evidence of progress from you to them.

I created a simple system called Make Me an Artist, which is an A4 sheet stuck at the back of sketchbooks. It has four headings that focus on knowledge learned, skills developed, creativity achieved and areas for improvement. At specific points in my lesson and curriculum, I ask pupils to turn to the sheet and copy a succinct sentence from the board that summarises a learning activity, for example '12th Feb we learned about the artist Mondrian' or '15th June we practised pencil shading'. In this way, they have a reminder of what they've done to look back on, which also acts as a consolidation memory exercise. The beauty of this, of course, is that you haven't done the work here – they have.

And that's it really! I hope that isn't too daunting, because art assessment should be a conversational dialogue aimed at improving the individual's confidence and giving them useful information for improvement, while still being manageable for the teacher and not increasing workload. Assessment in art is a classroom activity. Please avoid sticking onerous matrices, grids and descriptors in sketchbooks that only complicate the process and baffle everybody. If assessment makes me feel like I've failed at something and don't want to do it again, then it has been harmful. Sadly, there is too much assessment in schools that does that, and art and design should be such a rewarding and uplifting subject.

Source

Wiliam, D. (2014) 'Providing feedback that moves learning forward': a series of six lectures given by Dylan Wiliam for South Australia's Department of Education and Child Development [online] Available at: https://youtu.be/BUPuNc6iYj8?si=yAljTaMctCYG4lMZ (Accessed: 17 May 2026).

Assessment of art: Tyson Oliver (Art and DT Trust Lead) and Louisa Morris (Deputy Director of Education of Curriculum), Rise Academy Trust

Rationale

We regard art as an expressive and subjective form of communication; our aim is for pupils to develop a curiosity, appreciation and understanding of art in its various forms in different time, place and world contexts.

An ambitious art curriculum fills part of the cultural capital deficit that exists in our communities. Art makes a significant contribution to equality (Brett and Brassington, 2023); it enables our pupils to be part of the wider conversations; it encourages deep thinking and imagination for personal pleasure and for future innovation.

As a multi-academy trust, we have to take a position on what we want all our pupils to be able to experience and be confident in achieving by the end of their primary-school education. Our conversations with secondary colleagues have pointed out that many primary pupils have not had sufficient experience of engaging with art.

Formative assessment of art

Through expert questioning, formative assessment enables teachers to check pupil understanding quickly, identify misconceptions and adequately adapt teaching to the needs of their pupils. Quality feedback; models; and reflecting critically on their own work all help pupils develop their own sense of style as they craft and adapt pieces, moving from novice to expert.

Quizzing

Each unit of work consists of five to ten lessons; these are delivered in a block so, over the course of a week, pupils have five art lessons. Quizzing is an important part of our lesson structure; standardised quizzes have been designed to support pupils' acquisition of knowledge through retrieval practice and spaced learning. At the end of each lesson, pupils are asked one or two questions, which build over the course of the unit to 10 questions (see the following examples from a Year 4 Still Life and Form Unit), which pupils are able to answer confidently by the end.

1. What is a still life a picture of?
2. What are construction lines in art?
3. Name some line techniques.
4. Which civilisation is credited with creating the first still life?
5. Still-life artwork has been created for thousands of years: true or false?
6. What does *tone* mean?
7. What is cross-hatching?
8. What is Cézanne known for painting?
9. What is the shading technique that uses lines going in one direction?
10. What is the shading technique that uses lines that cross each other called?

Core content quizzes are spread through the year to allow pupils to return to previous learning to enable them to retrieve and strengthen knowledge.

Summative assessment

The end-of-unit assessment provides us with raw data against a standard benchmark; this keeps leaders informed of pupil progress and their trajectory in meeting their learning goals. It provides a trust-wide understanding of the extent to which the teaching and learning of art is equitable in all our schools. Assessment, then, helps us to ensure an ambitious curriculum is implemented effectively and that there are high expectations for all pupils.

How we assess

Our starting point for assessment is curriculum core content; that is, what our professional judgement tells us that our pupils need to know, understand and practise. Our assessment is informed by the seven elements of art: line, shape, space, value, form, texture and colour.

We assess both knowledge and skills, while accepting that these two concepts interlink and are equally important and not seen in isolation. We want our pupils to be able to develop their artistic skill but do so in a variety of ways using a variety of mediums.

Our curriculum is carefully sequenced and progressive so that pupils build on their prior knowledge. While the structure is important, we also encourage a balance of pupils' personal creativity and artistic exploration – our aim is not to have 400 sketchbooks and art portfolios looking the same.

We have produced a simple assessment guide for each teaching unit to support teacher assessment (see Table 10.1). The framework is best fit. By identifying core knowledge, skills and vocabulary that pupils need to know in each primary phase, we can support the incremental build of pupil understanding. Teachers use observation, pupil discussion and the work that is produced to give a rounded assessment of what a pupil has learned and understood.

▼ **Table 10.1 Supporting Teacher Assessment of non-core subjects: Art Year 3**

Unit 2: Landscapes
Core knowledge • Explore the work of Constable and Turner. • Landscapes can be created using different mediums. • Understand the term *perspective drawing* and how to apply its techniques to pupils' own drawing. • Salvador Dalí created landscapes using *surrealism*. • Develop a critical understanding of landscapes and further understanding of how to compare landscapes.

Unit 2: Landscapes
Artist skills • Accurately apply line to perspective drawings. • Apply different mediums to perspective drawings. • Create a surreal background and landscape using perspective. • Be able to compare and contrast works of art and artists.
Key vocabulary landscape mediums relate interpret perspective horizon technique vanishing point one-point perspective two-point perspective cube surreal background surrealism
Artists Constable Cézanne Monet Bruegel the Elder Leonardo da Vinci David Hockney Miro Salvador Dalí
Indications that a pupil is meeting age-related expectations • Shows understanding and is able to use key vocabulary • Is able to answer 70% of the cumulative core-content quizzes accurately • Is able to give simple answers and shows recognition of the core knowledge identified • Can give an opinion and compare and contrast some art • Is able to identify and talk about some of the artists above and their work • Is able to develop artist skills and processes – linking to previous knowledge and techniques
Exemplifications for age-related expectations Here we place links to exemplifications for age-related expectations for teachers to use as a guide for their assessments.

Impact

Our assessment framework has given teachers a rigorous tool that supports our ambition for the excellent teaching and learning of art. By setting out clear expectations and assessing against these, we know which schools, which classes and which pupils are flourishing in their artist development and where we need to direct further resource.

Assessment supports our relentless drive to increase the quality of teaching and learning of art. Our curriculum is recognised by stakeholders outside our trust as being influentially strong; our assessment framework helps us to secure this high standard of entitlement for all.

Summary

Assessing pupils' progress in primary art and design will never be straightforward, and this chapter makes no claim that it is. The individual, expressive, subjective nature of the subject sits very uncomfortably with the tidy numerical judgements that can be made in so many other areas of the primary curriculum. Any teacher who forces it into that mould is going to have to compromise either the assessment or the subject itself. But this chapter has shown that thorough, careful, ongoing assessment is possible, and that when done correctly it can be incredibly useful. Observe pupils while they work; listen to what they say; assess the journey their sketchbooks show, not just the final outcome; give feedback that is kind, specific and helpful; and, above all, remember that you are assessing pupils' progress, not just their attainment. It is harder than it is with some subjects, but that does not make the principles any less valid.

Source

Brett, A. and Brassington, J. (2023) *Pride and progress: making schools LGBT+ inclusive spaces*. London: SAGE Publications.

Further reading

Berger, R. (2003) *An Ethic of Excellence: Building a Culture of Craftsmanship with Students*. Portsmouth, NH: Heinemann.

Berger, R. (2012) Austin's Butterfly: Models, Critique, and Descriptive Feedback [Video]. EL Education. Available at: https://www.youtube.com/watch?v=E_6PskE3zfQ (Accessed: 23 July 2026).

Carney, P. (2018) *The Primary Art Book: Art for Children Aged 4–11*. Self-published.

Wiliam, D. (2018) *Embedded Formative Assessment*, 2nd edn. Bloomington, IN: Solution Tree Press.

CHAPTER 11
PRODUCTS AND PROJECTS

Primary-school timetables are full. Not just a little bit full; more like 'squeezing an elephant into a Smart car'-type full! Teachers are constantly juggling to fit everything in and, with English and maths ring-fenced time, it becomes a battle for the foundation subjects to commandeer the remaining hours. Art has to battle to take up space. At best, schools give it half a day a week, at worst it may only be given half a day each term! So, how can leaders add to the art provision their pupils devour, and celebrate the subject without overloading the timetable? Here are some tried and tested suggestions to pick and choose from.

Art assemblies

Adding art assemblies to termly rotas is an exciting way to enrich the art experience of pupils. They can be used as a retrieval exercise, a pre-teach session, a celebration, to teach a concept, introduce a new artist, read a new artwork, and more. During my time as Art Lead at Leighfield Primary School, art assemblies became embedded into our provision and the pupils gained so much in terms of knowledge and enjoyment from them.

Depending on the space available, the number of pupils and the amount of adult support on hand, it is an option to have shared drawing / making as part of these assemblies. Pupils can bring their sketchbooks and any drawing materials required and create together. In one such assembly I led, pupils drew self-portraits. We talked about the proportions and features of our faces and observed ourselves closely using mini mirrors, before embarking on the drawing experience. I modelled at the front of the hall using a visualiser and, step by step, we drew self-portraits. Another assembly, delivered during a cold winter spell, saw us studying how snow has been depicted in paintings throughout history; we explored the sixfold symmetry of snowflakes; and then designed our own. A favourite of mine, however, was one celebrating the life and achievements of Dame Vivienne Westwood, which included time for pupils to become fashion designers themselves, creating clothing designs for themselves in their sketchbooks. In our experience, pupils love the shared drawing experience and having discussions with peers from across the school during the creative process.

As staff, we were blown away by the pupils' focus, their resilience and their willingness to have a go in these assemblies. The sight of them all sitting, drawing, engrossed and absorbed in their creations was truly heart-warming. The outcomes were something else too. Even the very youngest in the school produced drawings that amazed us all, demonstrating the importance and effectiveness of incorporating modelling into a varied art provision. This shared experience was so successful we knew we had to provide more of the same, and thus art assemblies became a regular feature on our assembly rota.

Art assemblies don't always require creating or making. Many I have delivered were interactive but didn't include a shared drawing activity, such as one with a colour-theory focus, exploring warm and cool colours with EYFS and KS1. For the younger pupils, this was a pre-teach, something they had not yet been introduced to in school. For the older pupils, it was a chance to retrieve information they had been taught the previous year. It was interactive in the sense that pupils were asked to respond to colours and artworks and talk to those around them to share thoughts and feelings. This one also included a little sing-song with a lovely rendition of 'I can sing a rainbow'!

Subsequent assemblies focused on sketching skills, observational drawing, guest speakers and artist studies. While different in content, one thing they all had in common was the excited fist pumps into the air and whispered cheers as pupils entered the hall eager for the half hour ahead. Following the assemblies, pupils from across the school were keen to talk about art, share their artwork with staff and peers and discuss their creations. This initiative really helped embed a creative culture in school.

Assemblies can be linked to what is happening in the wider world or connected to themed days, weeks and months, such as World Book Day (remember that illustrators play just as important a role in picture books as the authors), British Science Week and Black History Month; national or international sporting occasions or successes; royal occasions and other notable community, local, national or world events make the perfect focus for art assemblies too.

Artist of the term

Some schools choose to celebrate artists throughout the year in addition to those already on their curricula, each term choosing an individual for each class to study. Art leaders may suggest particular artworks by the artist for each year group to focus on, and these explorations are shared towards the end of the term in an assembly. During the term, classes display the artwork in their classrooms or maybe even stick them on their doors so that the rest of the school, and visitors, can see their focus piece. School initiatives like this give pupils the opportunity to develop their visual literacy skills and the ability to compare and contrast artwork by the same artist, and provide a platform for them to express their likes and dislikes in relation to art. If pupils learn and talk about the artwork of one extra artist every term, that equates to three a year or 21 throughout their primary-school education.

Develop a culture of talking about art

Discuss likes and dislikes and admire work together. While pupils are carrying out art sessions, encourage teachers and support staff to join in and discuss the processes they are practising and the work they are creating. Art is for everyone, and conversations about it can and should transcend all age groups.

Run art clubs or workshops

Many schools run art clubs for their pupils, either after school or during lunch hour, depending on school context. Running such a club allows pupils with a particular interest, passion or aptitude for the subject to take part in additional sessions. The way these clubs are run varies – some may allow pupils the time and space to explore their own artist identities by providing (or making) sketchbooks, paper, tools and media for them to create and explore freely with. Others may be more structured, with a particular activity or focus planned for each week or term.

Inviting guests in to work with teachers to run art-club sessions acts as a source of inspiration for pupils and gives them the opportunity to partake in activities that would otherwise be unavailable due to lack of resources or in-house expertise. Local communities can be a real hidden treasure trove of artistic talent and support for schools. During my time as an art leader, we ran after-school creative workshops with pupils' friends and extended family members as the joint hosts alongside myself. These workshops ran for one hour at the end of the school day. I put the feelers out among the school and local community to find willing participants and was overwhelmed by the enthusiastic replies. A simple letter home brought in the response we were hoping for, and pupils benefited from a series of sessions by cake designers, architects, ceramicists, fashion illustrators, graphic designers, and more, which opened their eyes to a variety of creative careers and gave them the opportunity to learn from experts in their fields.

Whole-school events

As a school, you can work together to create something fabulous! Link your project to special events on your school calendar or theme your project to special national or international days or weeks such as World Oceans Week or World Book Day. Your classes can create work on the theme to display together in a whole-school gallery or create some big art, with every pupil contributing in some way. To celebrate the artwork created, you can invite parents / carers in to view the finished masterpieces and contact your local newspaper to share pupils' hard work and creativity with the community.

The National Gallery 'Take One Picture' Initiative has been inspiring schools and providing outstanding CPD for teachers since 1995, each year taking 'one picture' from its collection to encourage cross-curricular thinking and actions by primary pupils. Many schools choose to create their own art galleries, with each class creating a response to the chosen artwork. Previous focus artworks have included Henri Rousseau's 'Surprised!' (1891), Claude Joseph-Vernet's 'A Shipwreck in Stormy Seas' (1773) and Canaletto's 'A Regatta on the Grand Canal' (around 1740). It's up to individual schools how they run their 'Take One Picture' projects, but all are invited to submit work to the National Gallery to be exhibited at their show in London.

Invite practising artists into school

When pupils meet, see and learn directly from real-life artists in school, the experience can have a lasting impact on their career dreams and aspirations, in some cases opening up a whole new world of creative career options they may otherwise never have known existed. The NSEAD website includes an artist-educator directory that schools can use to help source visitors into schools. As the website explains, 'Artist Educators are artists who earn the majority of their income from professional artistic practice but also supplement their income by working as teaching artists. They may offer creative workshops, run whole school projects or provide specialist advice and inspiration for the whole curriculum.'

Visit galleries

Making links with local galleries is an invaluable way to bring art to life. There's nothing quite like seeing the actual strokes of paint on a canvas, the light shining off the surfaces of a sculpture or the fine, delicate marks of pencil on paper. Looking at art on a whiteboard screen, on a photocopy handout or on the pages of a book just simply does not do the works justice. Art is naturally linked to gallery settings, and teachers talk about them, assuming pupils have prior knowledge of the aims and purposes of such spaces, but many won't. A visit to a gallery with school may be the only time some pupils ever set foot in one. On a side note here, the picture book *Luna Loves Art* by Joseph Coelho and Fiona Lumbers (2021) is a great way to introduce young children to the concept of an art gallery.

While teaching in Uppingham, I made links with a beautiful local gallery, Goldmark Art, which, luckily for us, was only a short walk away from school. Each academic year, two year groups visited the gallery, one being EYFS and the other whichever year's art curriculum most closely aligned with the gallery exhibitions. Pupils loved looking slowly and closely at the artworks and discussing them with their peers; some of the conversations I overheard were truly magical and heartwarming. There's nothing quite like hearing five-year-olds enjoying noticing details and comparing artworks unprompted! On return to school, one EYFS class were so inspired by what they saw that they chose to create a gallery for their parents / carers to visit at pick-up time. They spent a whole afternoon excitedly painting and displaying their work for others to see.

Another, often easy, way to access art is to visit a local high school or college where students may be displaying their own pieces. This serves multiple purposes, as older pupils know their work will be visited, and younger pupils can see a wide range of work displayed, as well as have art role-modelled by an older pupil. If you do not have a gallery space locally, some local amateur art groups are often happy to visit school and set up a pop-up gallery or bring along lots of examples of their work for pupils to see. Establishing links with local amateur groups is also a great way to show how art can be a wonderful lifelong endeavour.

Display and celebrate

Art is created to be viewed and admired. Creating galleries in the classroom and in other spots around school develops pupils' self-esteem, pride in their work and confidence. Empty frames ready hung provide easy-to-fill spaces so, as soon as artwork is complete, it can be placed quickly on the wall and celebrated. When it's time to refresh the gallery, the frames are there ready to be emptied and refilled! Pupils love to see their work on display and enjoy discussing both their own work and that of their peers. The display's story can accompany it: Who created it? What was the context? There are also apps available for creating online galleries, which can be shared with parents / carers or on social media. A school adorned in art displays sends a message to every visitor that art is valued and appreciated.

Create a school art council

An art council can run in a similar way to a general school council, with representatives from each year group involved, the aim being for pupils involved to share their own, and their classmates', voices to enhance the school-art provision in general and the learning taking place in class. Pupils love to belong to a club, especially when it's to do with a subject they enjoy and there's the prospect of being awarded a badge for being a member!

The way to start is to advertise:

> **Calling all KS2 Pupils!**
>
> *Do you enjoy creating art?*
>
> *Do you like talking about art?*
>
> *Do you love looking at art?*
>
> *Do you have ideas that will help improve the art experience of the pupils in our school?*
>
> If you answered **YES** to any of the questions above, would you like to become a member of the [insert school name] Art Council?
>
> Collect an application form from [insert teacher name] and return it by [insert date] to register your interest.

Pupils can apply for a position on the council and be encouraged to think about the strengths and skills they can bring to such a team. Art councils can meet as often as a school sees fit: once a week, once a fortnight, half termly, termly – there is no one-size-fits-all approach.

The council can decide on whole-school art projects together, plan schedules and work towards goals. Projects could be linked to whole-school themes; sourcing visitors, trips and workshops; choosing new equipment; running competitions; and more!

Include art and design in the school newsletter

Whether your school newsletters are weekly, monthly or termly, add a special section to celebrate art in your school. You may wish to focus on the learning of a particular class, the achievements of a particular pupil or the current art-council project. Sharing your arty news with parents / carers will undoubtedly encourage discussion on the subjects with their children at home and highlight to families that art and design is an important and valued aspect of school life.

- 'I loved it at the gallery! My favourite sculpture was of a dog.'
- 'It was an exciting trip. I loved taking photos. My favourite piece was the painting of a boat.'
- 'There were lots and lots of colourful paintings – I loved it!'
- 'I liked the bird sculptures; they made me smile!'

Summer-holiday art challenge

Many pupils get excited by the prospect of a holiday challenge, and feedback from parents / carers implies that they often appreciate the focus it gives them! Pupils may or may not have the resources at home to carry out the tasks, so schools can create packs for those who want to take part. Offering a sketchbook-making club during a lunchtime prior to the holidays is also a fun option for the artists in school.

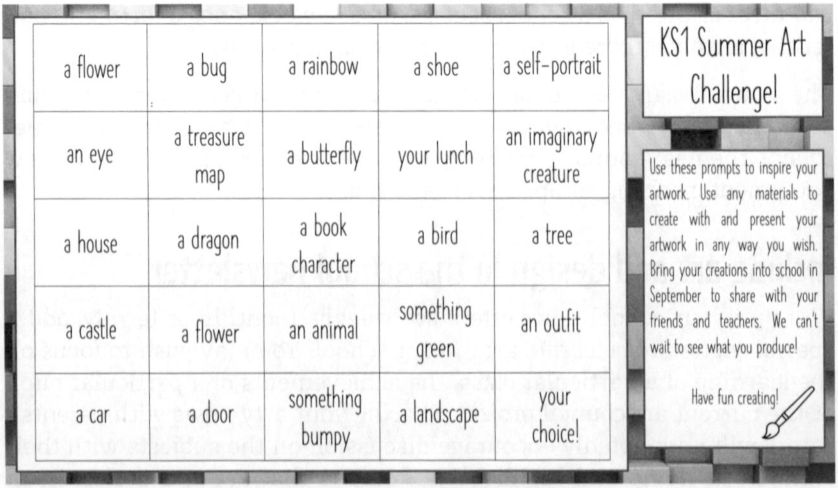

▲ **Figure 11.1 An example of a key stage 1 summer art challenge**

Make links across the curriculum

Raise awareness of the value of art and design across the curriculum by drawing attention to the role of art for different purposes. Highlight anatomical drawings and their importance in science, the role of map-drawing in geography, the value of the illustrations in picture books, drawings and paintings as source material in history – the links across the curriculum are too many to mention!

Summary

The common thread running through each suggestion in this chapter is one simple belief: that art and design is worthy of more than a half-hour slot squeezed into a packed timetable. Assemblies, clubs, councils and exhibitions allow you to demonstrate that belief to pupils, parents / carers and the world beyond. You may not have the resources to do all these things at once. That's fine. Select the two or three that suit your context and get cracking. The next chapter picks up on the final strand: ensuring that art and design weaves meaningfully through the rest of the curriculum, so that the subject enriches, and is enriched by, everything else pupils learn at school.

Further reading

AccessArt: Inspiring the Teaching and Learning of Visual Arts [online] Available at: www.accessart.org.uk (Accessed: 16 May 2026).

Artsmark (Arts Council England): The Creative Quality Standard for Schools [online] Available at: www.artsmark.org.uk (Accessed: 18 May 2026).

Coelho, J. and Lumbers, F. (2021) *Luna Loves Art*. London: Andersen Press.

Cultural Learning Alliance: Championing the Right to Art and Culture for Every Child [online] Available at: www.culturallearningalliance.org.uk (Accessed: 18 May 2026).

Tambling, P. and Bacon, S. (2023) *The Arts in Schools: Foundations for the Future*. London: A New Direction and Calouste Gulbenkian Foundation [online] Available at: www.anewdirection.org.uk/the-arts-in-schools (Accessed: 18 May 2026).

CHAPTER 12
LINKS WITH OTHER SUBJECTS

The discipline of art is wide reaching, its many facets touching spaces across all areas of the curriculum. It can be used to inspire, to enhance, to teach and add meaning to every subject. Art is a tool that teachers can use to illustrate concepts and ideas, share visual representations and offer alternative presentation methods to their pupils. It isn't just a subject to be confined to its own, one-hour-a-week box, but one that can weave its way intentionally and purposefully throughout the whole curriculum.

Music, dance and drama

Obvious links connect the world of the visual arts with the other creative subjects of music, dance and drama, all offering pupils valuable opportunities for self-expression. They co-exist beautifully in the primary classroom and there are ample opportunities for pupils to engage in them together. Careful planning can lead to exciting and enriching experiences for all. Some examples to try include:

- **adding a soundtrack to artwork:** By adding music or sounds to a piece of artwork, it is turned into a multisensory viewing experience. Sculptures of the ocean can be complemented by the sound of the waves, portraits of a class accompanied by the sound of playground chatter or paintings of nature displayed alongside the sound of birds tweeting.
- **creating in response to a piece of music:** Pupils can draw, paint or sculpt while listening; moving and making marks however they wish, in any way the music makes them feel.
- **creating a soundtrack to match a painting:** This may be a series of sounds such as footsteps or instrumental music.
- **interpreting an artwork through drama and dance:** After studying and discussing a piece together in class, pupils can work in groups to respond through movement and dialogue, with or without props.

History

The subject of history has long drawn on the power of art to discover and explore aspects of life in the past, with drawings, paintings, sculptures and other artistic forms providing invaluable windows into the world of times gone by. The role of art as a historical source is one that many take for granted but don't really give credit to the artists for their impact on life today. Some examples of how art can be used in primary history lessons include:

- **using artwork as a historical source:** Henry Moore's sketches of Londoners in underground stations in World War II give an insight into the conditions and experiences people were subjected to at that time. Artworks such as van Gogh's 'The Potato Eaters' (1885) can be explored and, in this case, an awareness raised of the life of a peasant family of the time. Zooming in to the details of this painting, such as the utensils on the table, the potatoes, the light source, the dark, dull conditions and solemn faces give an insight into their world.
- **looking not just at how art portrayed accurate representations but also how art was used in history to send a message:** For example, the grand and powerful portrayal of Henry VIII, who used portraiture to illustrate his power and wealth, and also the role of the portrait in the relationship between Anne of Cleves and Henry VIII (Henry agreeing to marry Anne of Cleves based on her appearance in a portrait, which some say was not an accurate representation); or in the use of Victorian still life, with its associated symbolism of fruit, flowers, opulence, trade and empire.
- **using art as a presentation method:** Give pupils the opportunity to present their work artistically, adding illustrations to topic work to demonstrate an understanding of their learning visually.

Science

The 'Flowers: Flora in Contemporary Art & Culture' (2025) exhibition at the Saatchi Gallery on King's Road, London highlighted beautifully the connection between art and science. Alongside the many modern depictions of plants and flowers sat the accurate, intricately detailed botanical artworks of artists such as Elizabeth Blackwell (1699–1758), who drew and coloured medicinal plants that featured in her book entitled *A Curious Herbal*. Alongside the illustrations, Blackwell wrote of the medicinal qualities of plants, which was of invaluable use to doctors and chemists. Botanical art has, and still does, play a critical role in detailing and classifying plant species all over the world, with artists capturing the features of the plants they study with absolute precision.

With similar attention to detail, anatomical artists create artworks of the structures of the body and its functions with scientific accuracy. Renaissance artist Leonardo da Vinci is arguably the best known of this genre, dissecting corpses to inform his artwork. Such artistic studies have contributed to the advance in understanding of the workings of the human body.

Alongside these valuable links between art and science, it's also important to mention in this section the concept of the scientific diagram. Such diagrams have their own unique style and purpose, which is very different from the artwork pupils encounter on the art and design curriculum. It is still drawing, but drawing for a different purpose.

English

Art naturally occupies numerous spaces in the primary English curriculum, be it as a storytelling medium, a source of writing inspiration or a process to help the development of ideas.

Pictures tell stories, and illustrators play a powerful role in the depiction of a narrative without the need for words. Wordless picture books such as *Tuesday* and *Flotsam* by David Weisner and *Journey* by Aaron Becker highlight the power of the illustration. Such books tell complete stories with beginnings, middles and ends, both vividly and successfully, without one single word. Using the illustrations in books, pupils can tell a story and notice details, improving their inference, comprehension and visual literacy skills.

Artwork can be used as a stimulus for writing across different genres. Paintings, drawings, sculptures and photographs can all inspire pupils to write.

The process of drawing images can help pupils to develop ideas for their writing too. The Centre for Literacy in Primary Education (CLPE)'s 'Power of Pictures' research (2021) highlighted a link between creativity, drawing and writing; it found that drawing had a real impact on the richness of independent writing, helping pupils to develop, play with and extend their ideas.

Religious education

Religions worldwide communicate and represent their ideologies through art, which may be symbolic, share a belief, depict a religious story or be a form of celebration. As part of the RE curriculum, pupils should be introduced to all these forms: recognising the symbols associated with the world's main religions; exploring religious artworks and reading the messages within them; and learning about how art is associated with many festivals worldwide. They should also recognise art's role in conveying ideas about religion and belief before most people could read, and about how its use varies between different religions.

Geography

Art can be used to bring the subject of geography to life, giving depth and meaning to the content covered in all year groups. It can help pupils visualise concepts, develop geographical thinking and retain knowledge. Here are some ways art can be incorporated into geography lessons:

- Using paintings, drawings and sculptures to illustrate the various human and physical geographical features of the world, such as a painting of a landscape or a model of a town
- Using photography both as a means of illustrating elements of the curriculum and as a method of capturing moments, landmarks and geographical features on field studies
- Maps are integral to the study of geography and a unique, subject-specific art form; orienteering activities are a fun way for pupils to develop map-reading skills; drawing maps of the local area, journeys to school and of the classroom or school grounds are simple ways of introducing their features to pupils
- Presenting research and explorations in artistic forms, such as 3D models of landscapes.

Maths

The world of mathematics and art are entwined in so many ways. Geometry, symmetry, ratio, pattern, shape and tessellation are some of the key mathematical concepts that present in visually pleasing artistic forms. This link between the subjects paves the way for interesting, accessible and practical teaching and learning. The following art activities, artists and artworks can be used to reinforce links with maths:

- **Shape:** Artists and artworks to share with pupils include Paul Klee's 'Castle and Sun' (1928), Piet Mondrian's 'Composition with Large Red Plane, Yellow, Black, Grey and Blue' (1921), Sonia Delaunay's 'Electric Prisms' (1914), Alma Thomas' 'Lunar Rendezvous – Circle of Flowers' (1969) and Benode Behari Mukherjee's 'Two Triangles' (1957). Such artworks can be used as a starting point for discussions around shape and pattern and to inspire pupil creations in the classroom.
- **Symmetry:** Printing is an effective way to introduce and demonstrate mirror symmetry to young pupils, with pupils painting on one side of a piece of paper and folding down a central line to print a reflected image on the other side.
- **Patterns in nature:** The natural world is home to some of the most beautiful patterns. Some of those introduced in maths lessons can be found outside. Pupils can go on pattern hunts to look for examples of symmetry, such as on leaves, butterflies and insects. They can study the spirals of snails, demonstrating the Fibonacci sequence, or the hexagonal tessellation of honeycomb. The macro artworks of photographer Levon Biss demonstrate close up the intricate symmetry of minibeasts and can be used to inspire artistic responses from pupils.

Design and technology

Art and design and design and technology both have the word 'design' in their names, but it is important that schools treat them as individual subjects. They are not the same, despite this obvious commonality.

- *Design* in **design and technology** works towards a functional outcome. The design is a response to a need identified in a brief for a particular user and purpose, such as designing a healthy snack for children to eat at a picnic.
- *Design* in **art and design** is more aesthetic by nature, such as designing a pattern for wallpaper.

Design and technology projects must always have a product, user and purpose, which is something that art and design projects do not always require. Saying this, the two subjects can work alongside each other well and with elements of one spilling over into the other. Artistic skills, techniques and knowledge can be used when considering the aesthetic qualities of products created in DT lessons.

Conclusion

Art does not exist in isolation. It is just as much at home in the music room, in the history corner, in the science investigation, in the English lesson and on the maths carpet as it is in its own allotted weekly time on the timetable. Every area of the primary curriculum has something to teach about art, and everything art teaches can enrich lessons across the school. Whether that is illustration as a gateway into writing, observational drawing as a method for scientific precision or pattern and symmetry at the crossroads of art and maths, the teachers who embrace these opportunities do not dilute art and design by sharing it across the curriculum; they enhance it by giving pupils multiple opportunities to learn that art is one of the ways the world makes sense of itself.

It is this belief that underscores every word of this book: that primary art and design can be rigorous, can be joyful and is worthy of every minute it gets, both in its own subject lessons and in its partnerships with every other subject pupils learn about at school. Where the important work of teaching art goes next is up to you, the teachers, leaders and pupils who continue this work in your own classrooms.

Further reading

Becker, A. (2014) *Journey*. London: Walker Books.

Blackwell, E. (1737–1739) *A Curious Herbal*. London: John Nourse.

Centre for Literacy in Primary Education (2021) 'Power of Pictures' [online] Available at: https://clpe.org.uk/research/power-pictures-research-evaluation-report-rsaeef-2021 (Accessed: 18 May 2026).

Weisner, D. (2012) *Flotsam*. London: Andersen Press.

Weisner, D. (2012) *Tuesday*. London: Andersen Press.

Acknowledgements

The Publishers would like to thank the following for permission to reproduce copyright material.

pp.iii & 33–4 Quotes reproduced by permission of Kelvin Okafor; **p.5** Quote reproduced by permission of Ruth Millington; **p.6** Quote reproduced by permission of Sidney Taylor-Pettener; **p.6** Quote reproduced by permission of Stuart Jarvis; **pp.6–7 & 37–8** Excerpts from *Art and design programmes of study: key stages 1 and 2*, Department for Education, 2013 (https://assets.publishing.service.gov.uk/media/5a7ba810ed915d4147621ca0/PRIMARY_national_curriculum_-_Art_and_design.pdf). Contains public sector information licensed under the Open Government Licence v3.0. (https://www.nationalarchives.gov.uk/doc/open-government-licence/version/3/); **pp.15, 77–81 & 129** Excerpts reproduced by permission of Haringey Education Partnership; **p.15** Quote reproduced by permission of Simone Maier and NSEAD; **p.17** Extract reproduced by permission of Jenny Grevatte; **p.22** Quote reproduced by permission of Alex Quigley; **pp.22–4** References to *Research review series: art and design*, Ofsted, 2023 (https://www.gov.uk/government/publications/research-review-series-art-and-design/research-review-series-art-and-design). Contains public sector info licensed under the Open Government Licence v3.0. (https://www.nationalarchives.gov.uk/doc/open-government-licence/version/3/); **p.37** Quote reproduced by permission of Mary Myatt; **pp.44–9** Tables reproduced by permission of Mandy Barrett and Gomersal Primary School; **pp.49–57** Case study reproduced by permission of Karl Duke and Blyton cum Laughton CofE Primary School; **pp.57–61** Case study reproduced by permission of Rachel A. MacInnes and St Paul's Catholic Primary School; **pp.61–8** Case study reproduced by permission of Charlotte Ford, The Flying High Trust and Cotgrave Candleby Lane School; **pp.61 & 67** Excerpts from Ofsted's inspection report on Cotgrave Candleby Lane School, Ofsted, December 2023 (https://reports.ofsted.gov.uk/provider/21/138353). Contains public sector information licensed under the Open Government Licence v3.0. (https://www.nationalarchives.gov.uk/doc/open-government-licence/version/3/); **pp.130–40** Case study reproduced by permission of Paul Carney; **pp.140–43** Case study reproduced by permission of Tyson Oliver and Rise Academy Trust; **p.149** Excerpt from *NSEAD Artist Educator Directory*, NSEAD. Available at: https://www.nsead.org/community-activism/nsead-directories/. Reproduced by permission of NSEAD.